COLORING BOOK

for When You're Expecting

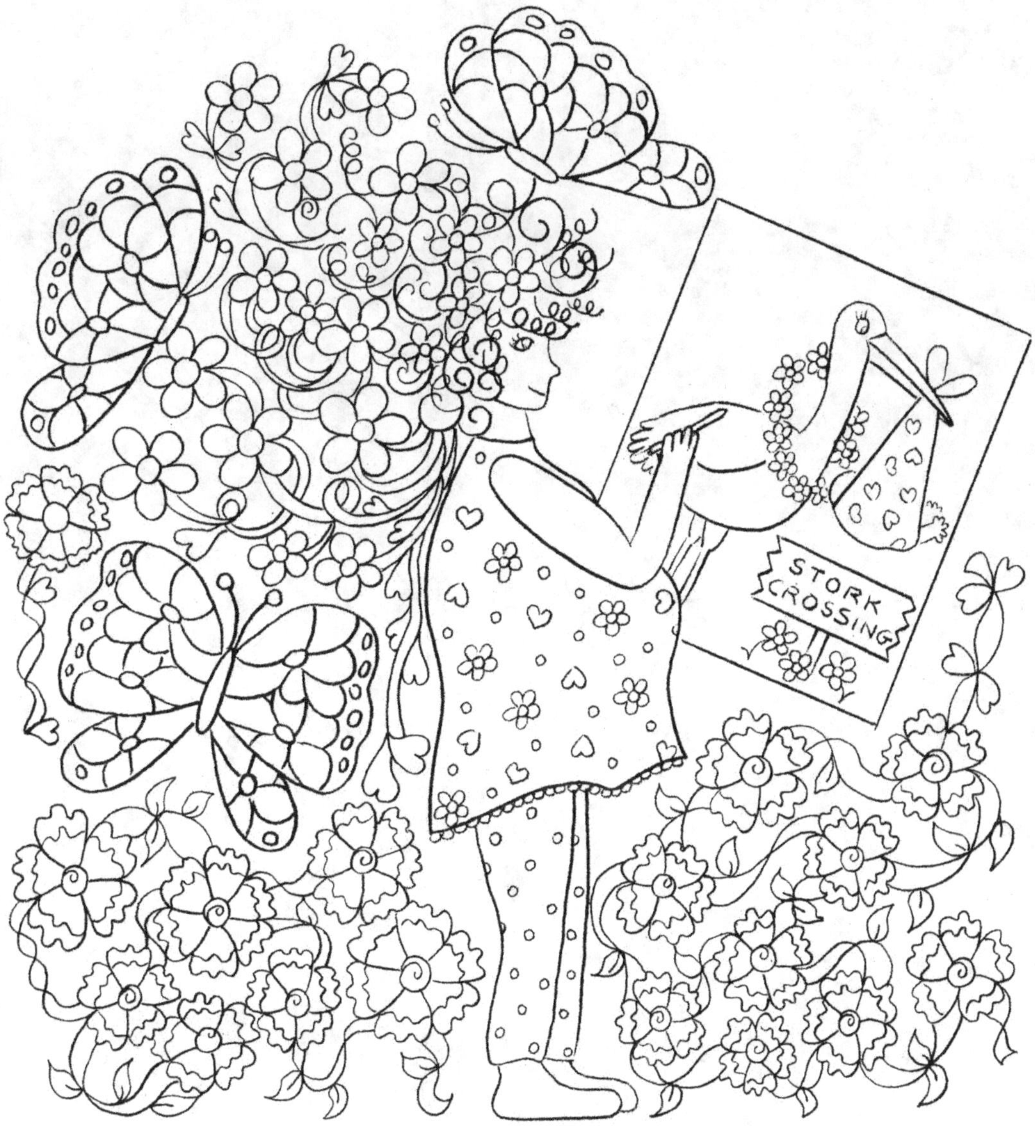

Jenny Pearson

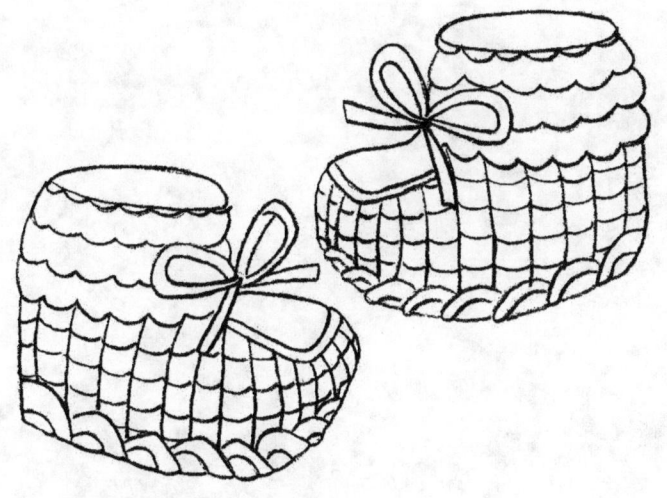

Coloring Book for When You're Expecting
Jenny Pearson

Kivett Publishing
ISBN: 978-1540665874

Arts & Photography > Drawing > Coloring Books

INTRODUCTION

These designs are the creation of artist Jenny Pearson.

Sit back, relax, and relieve some stress. Enjoy!

Note: For those who prefer to color with markers, the back side of every page is blank.

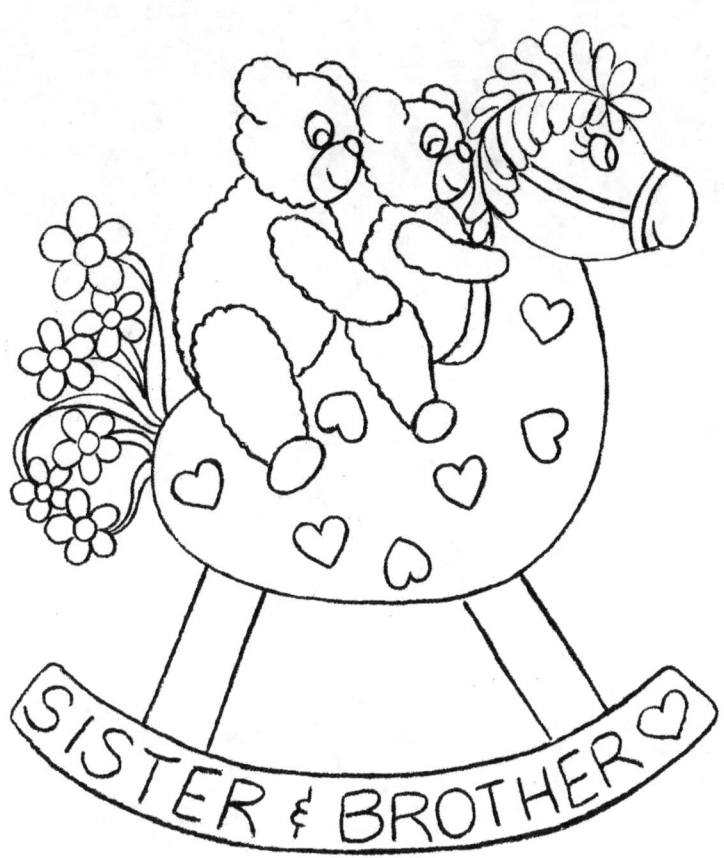

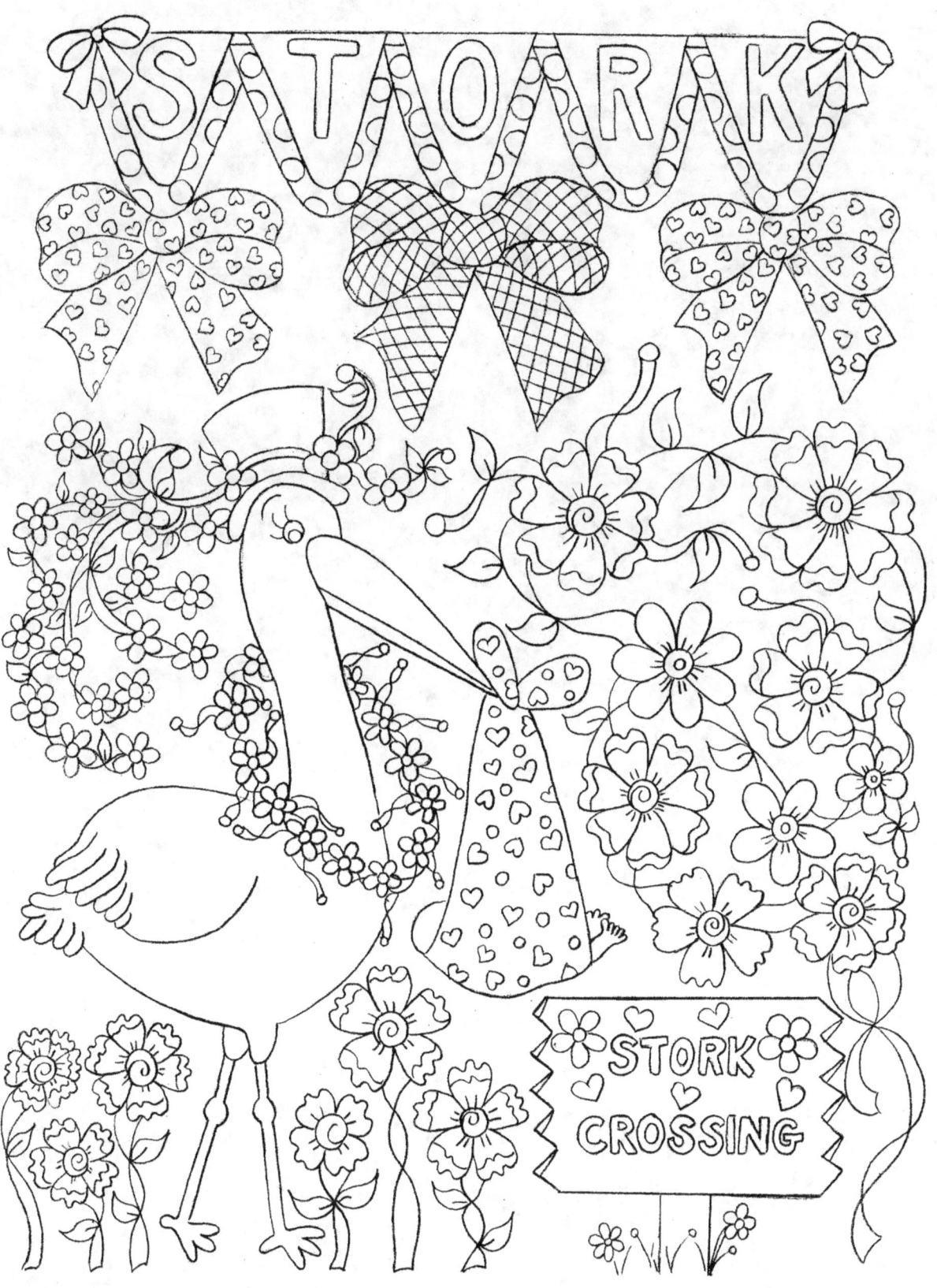

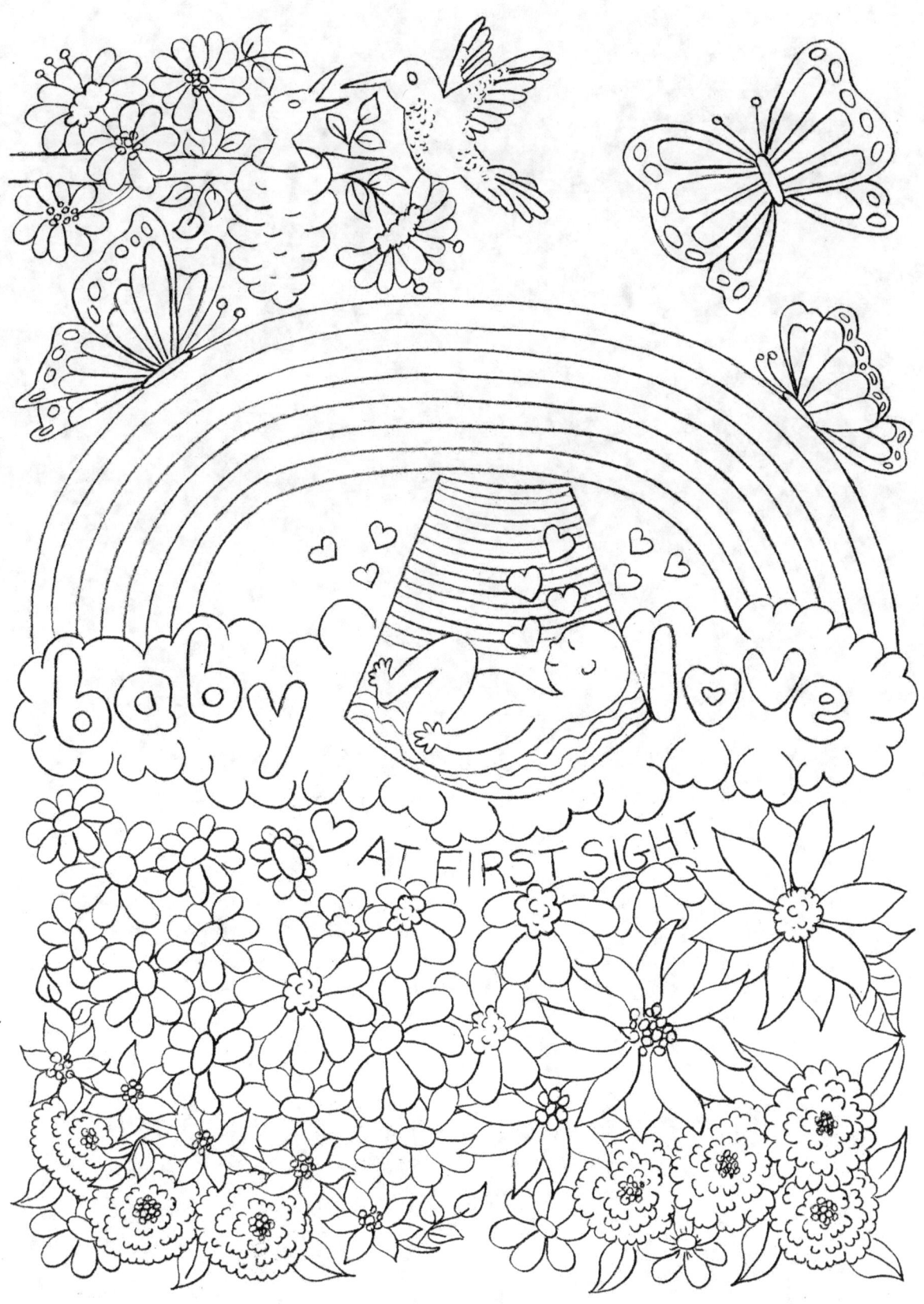

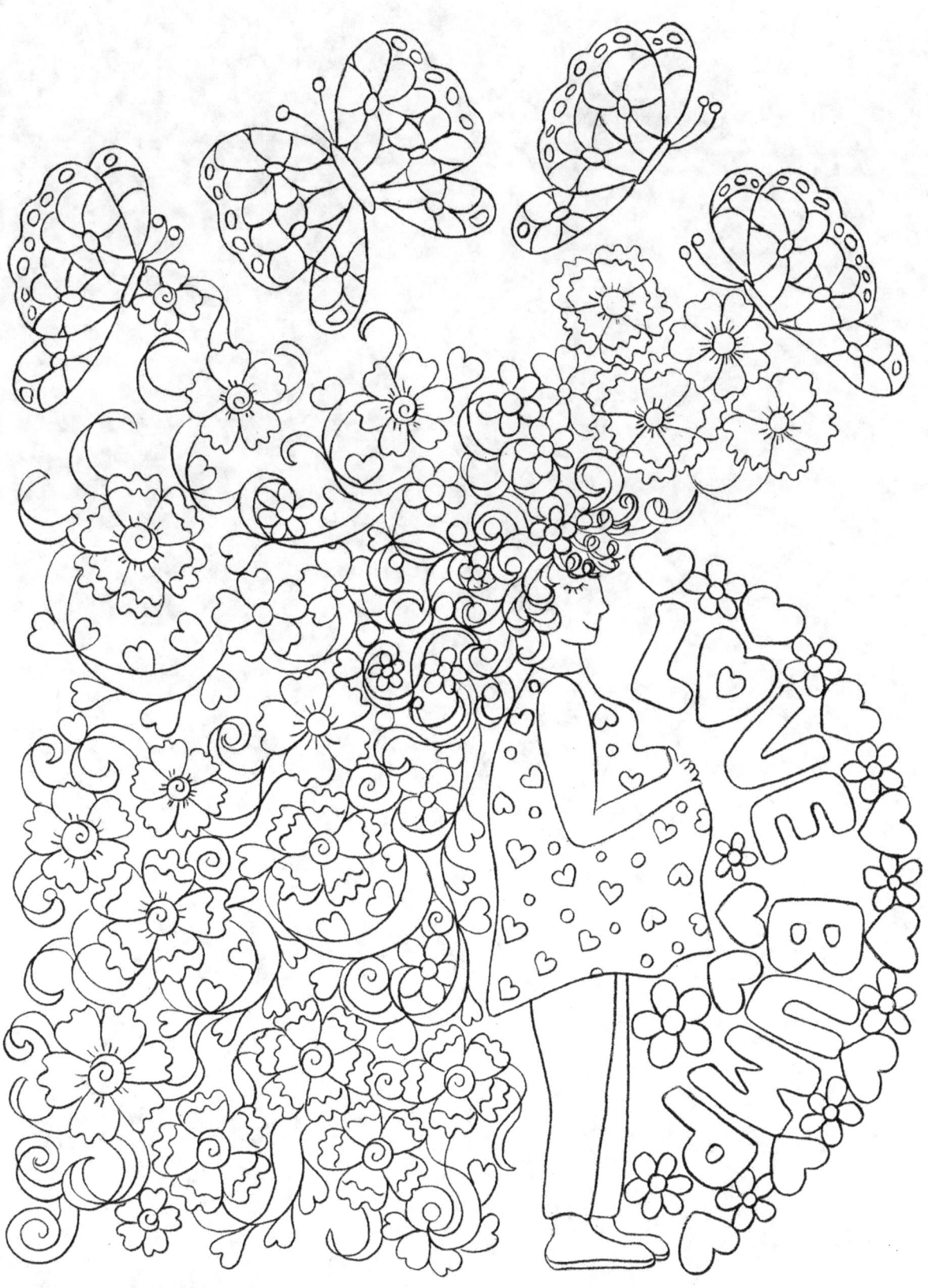

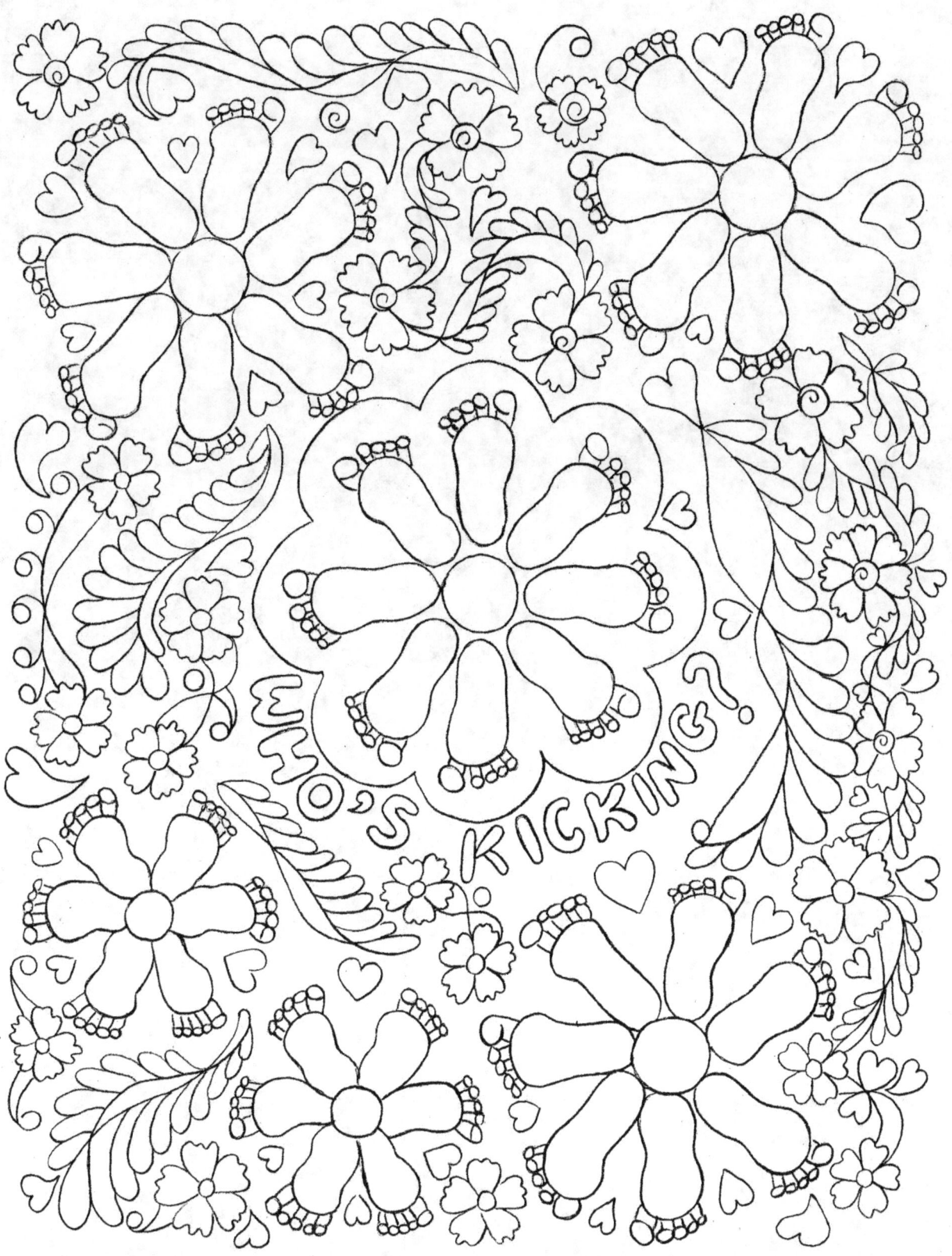

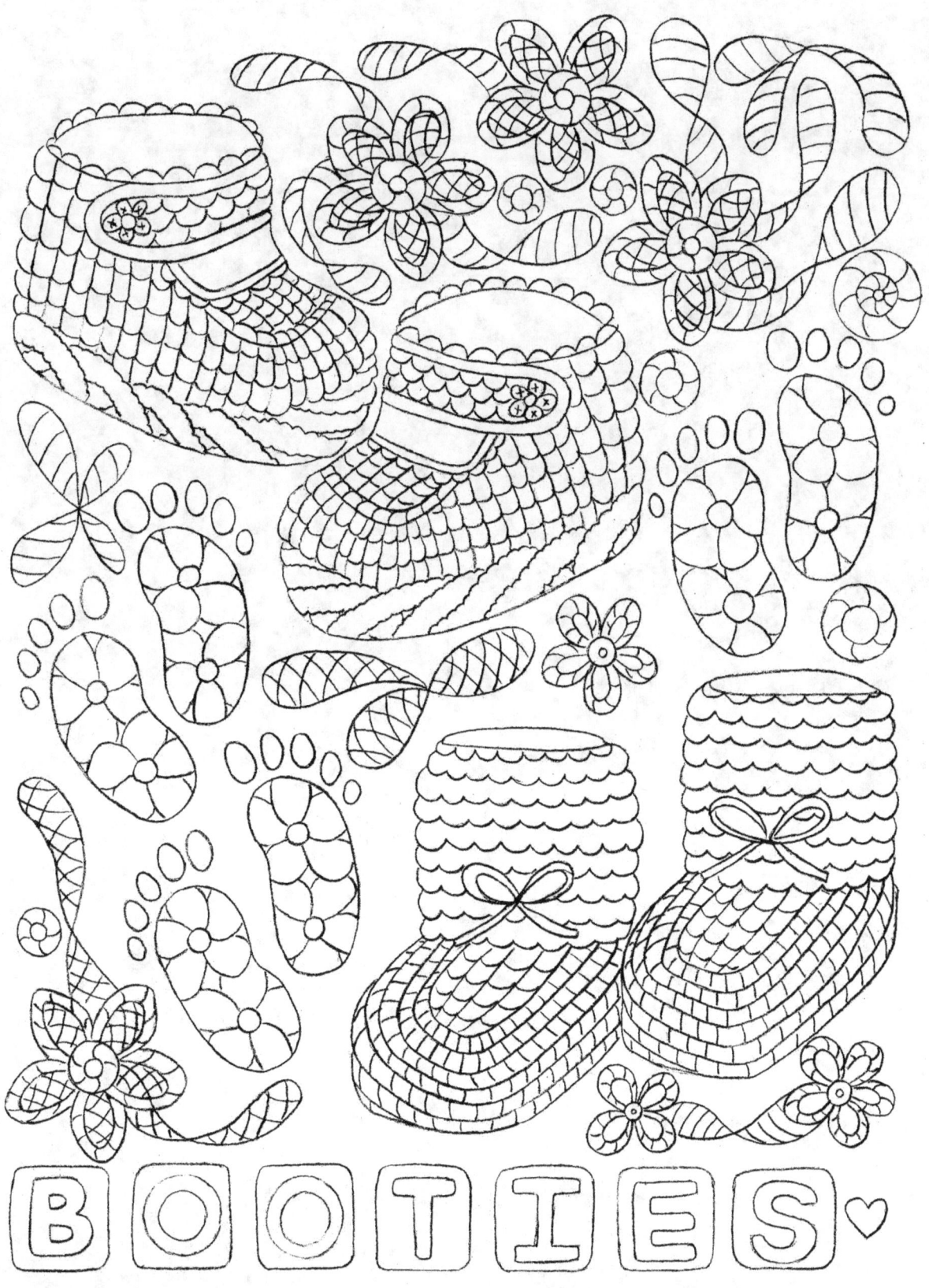

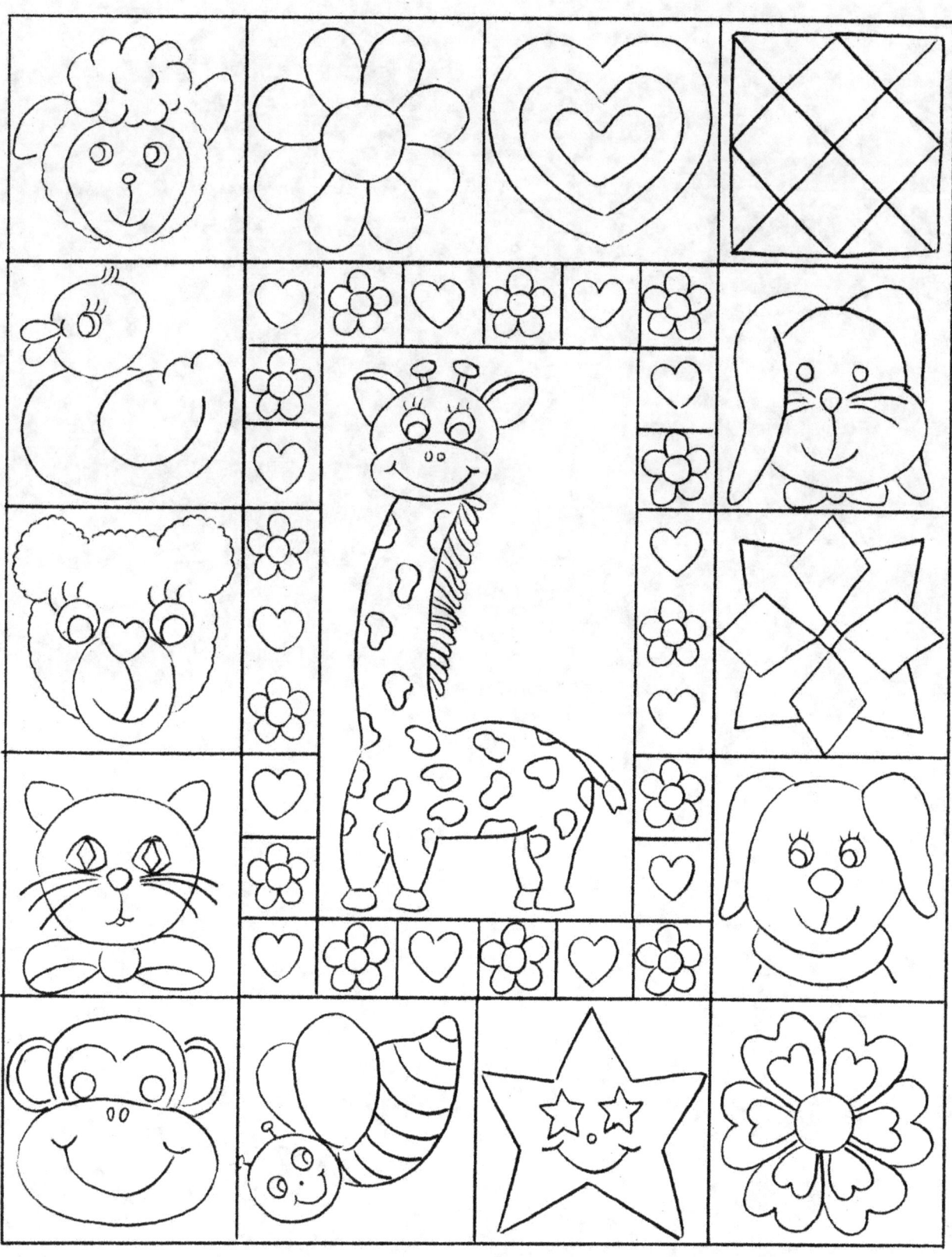

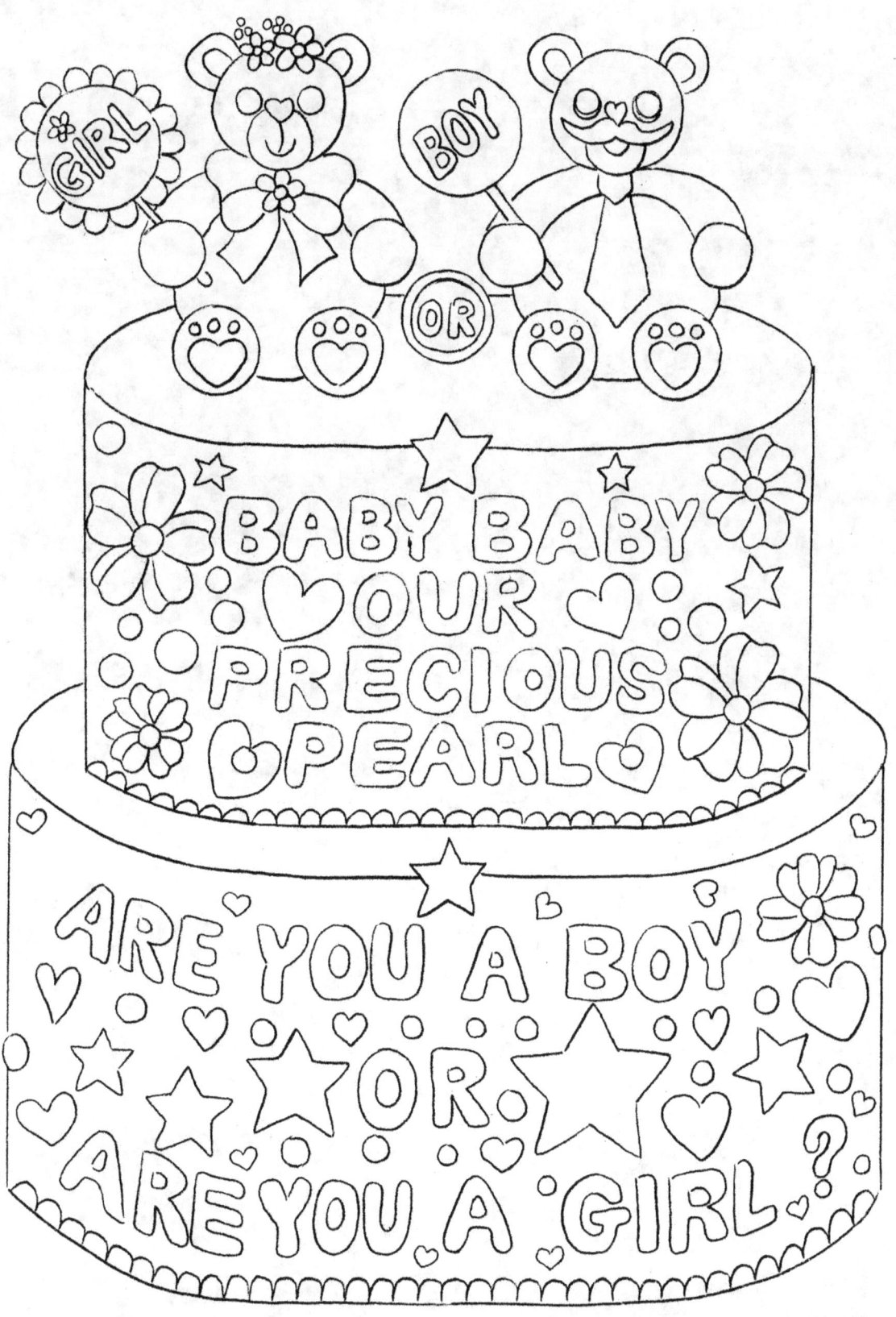

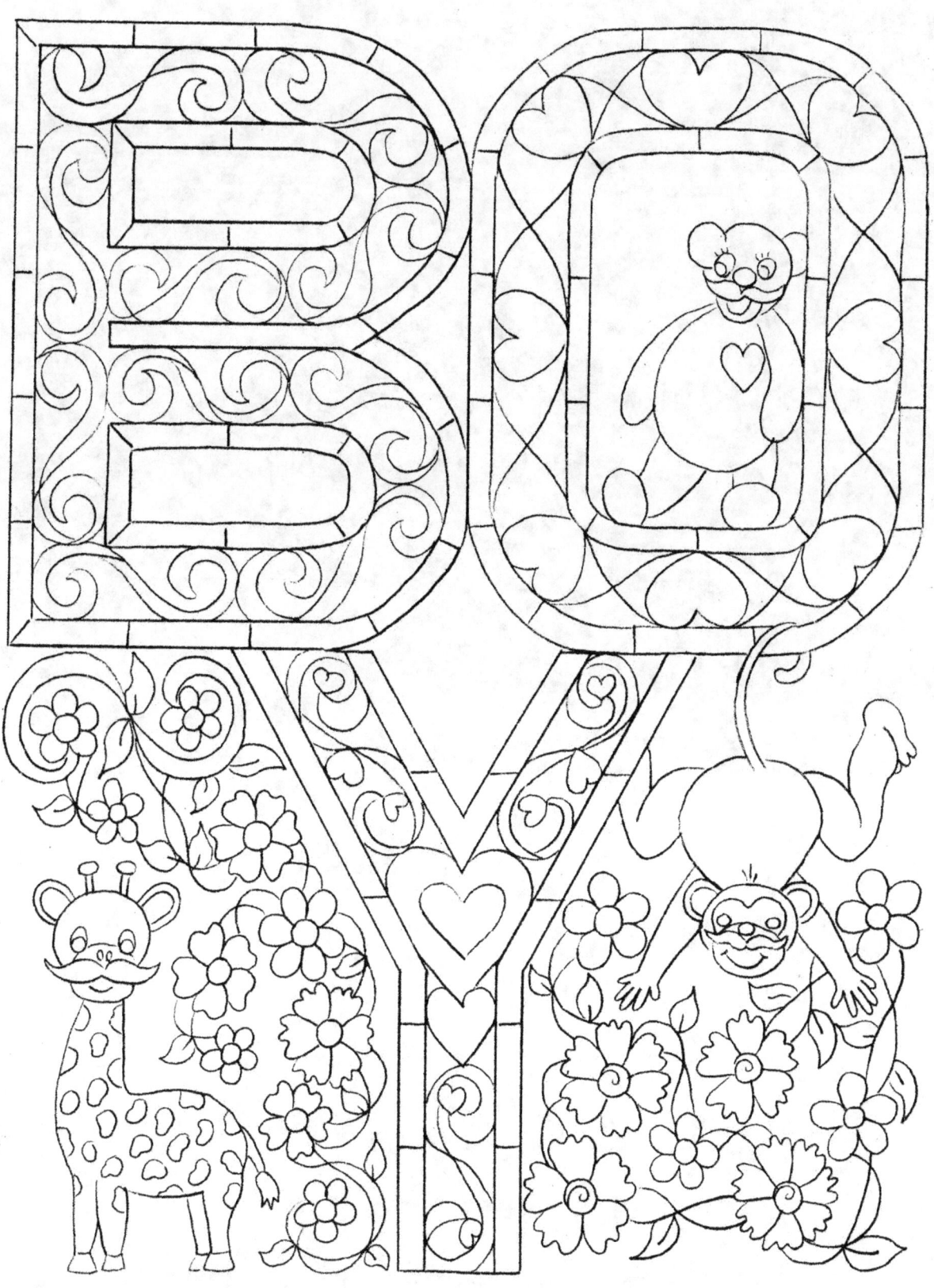

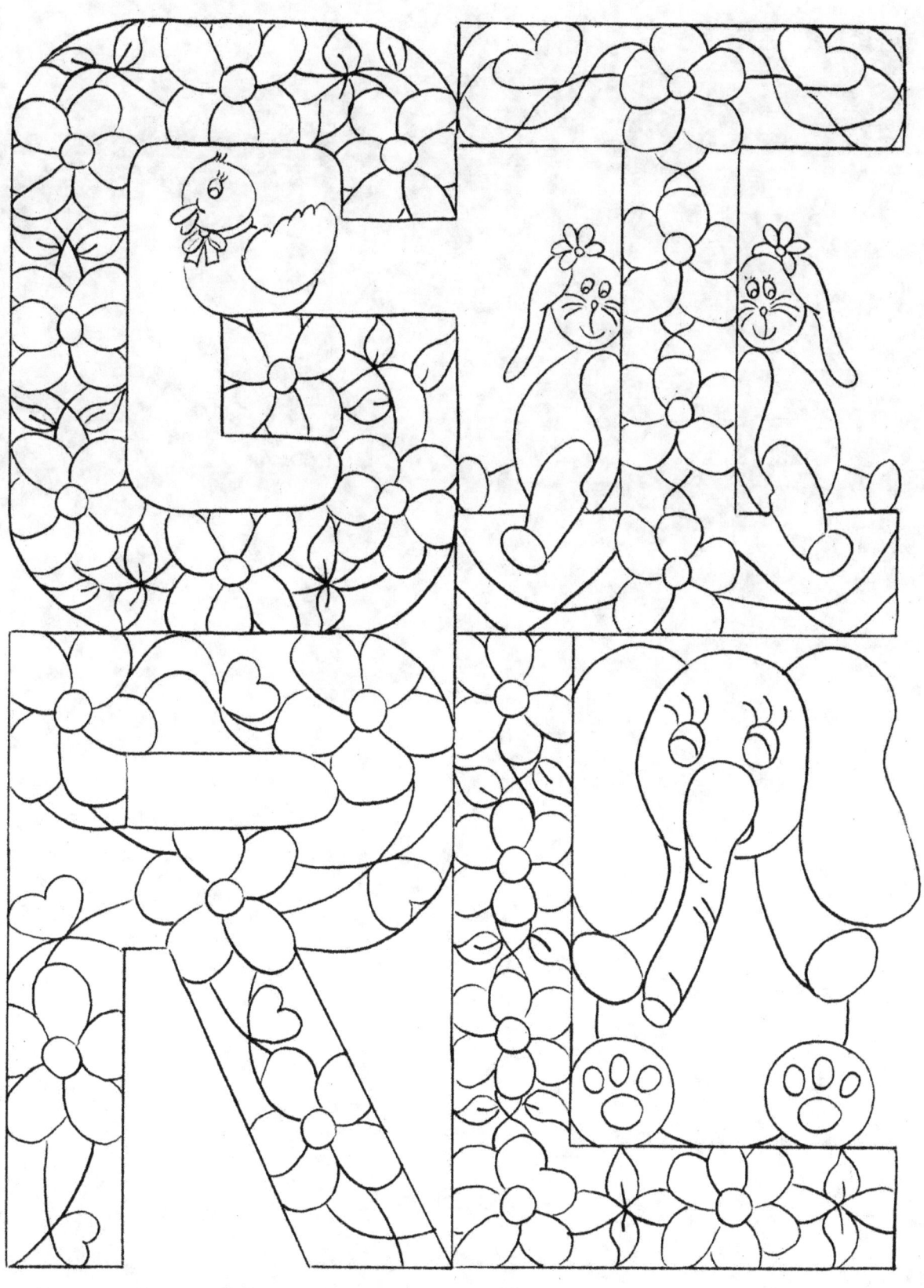

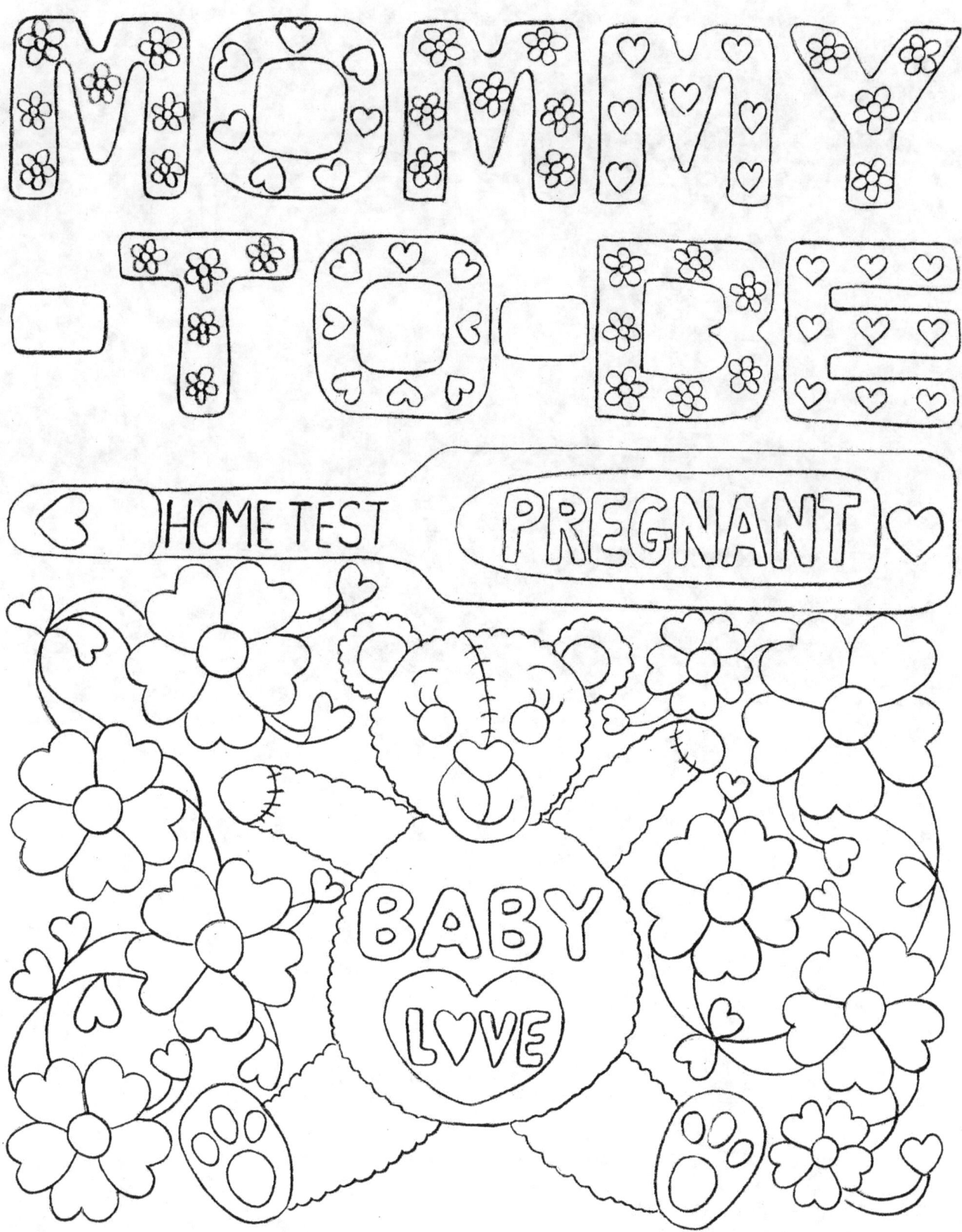

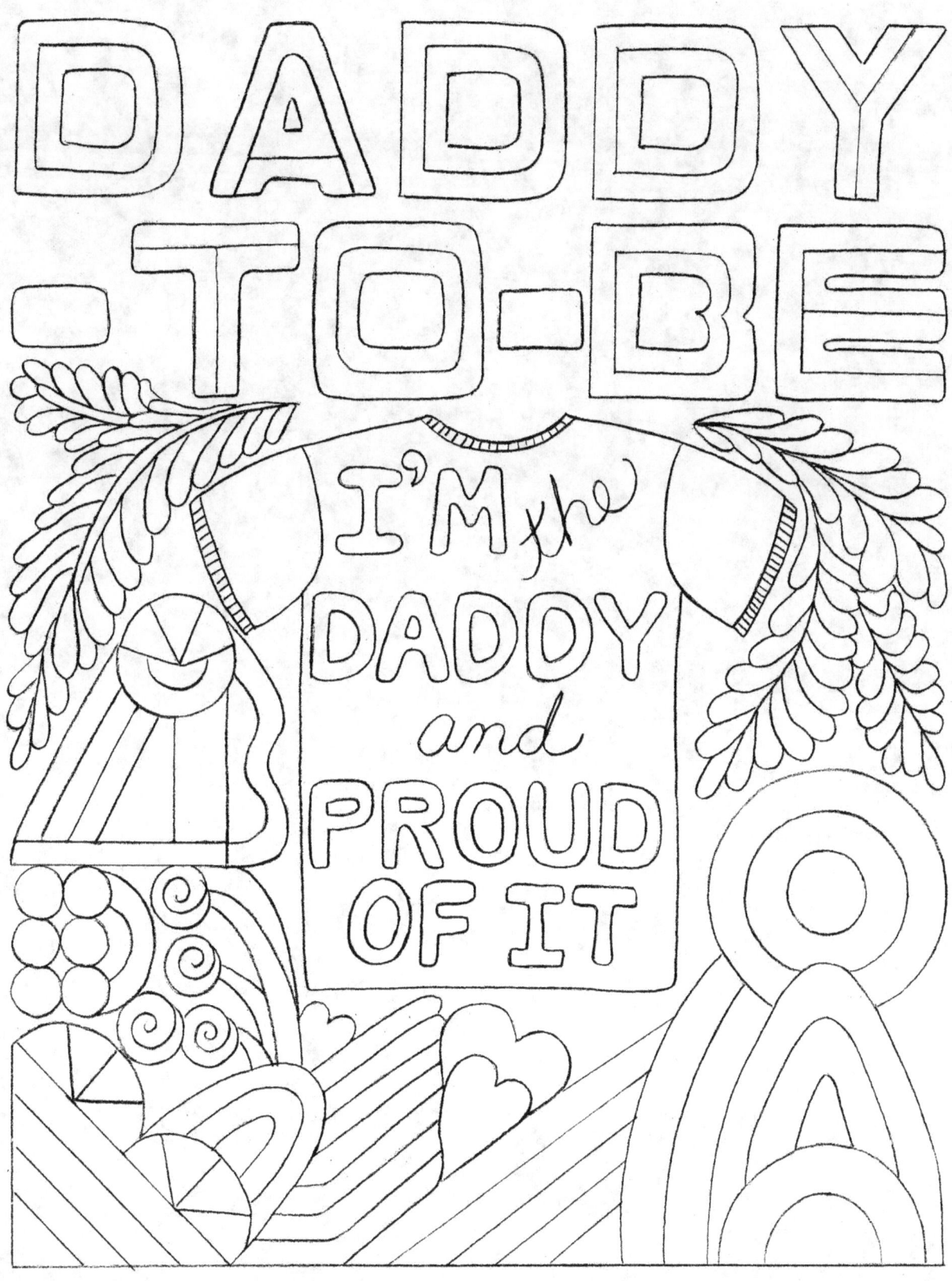

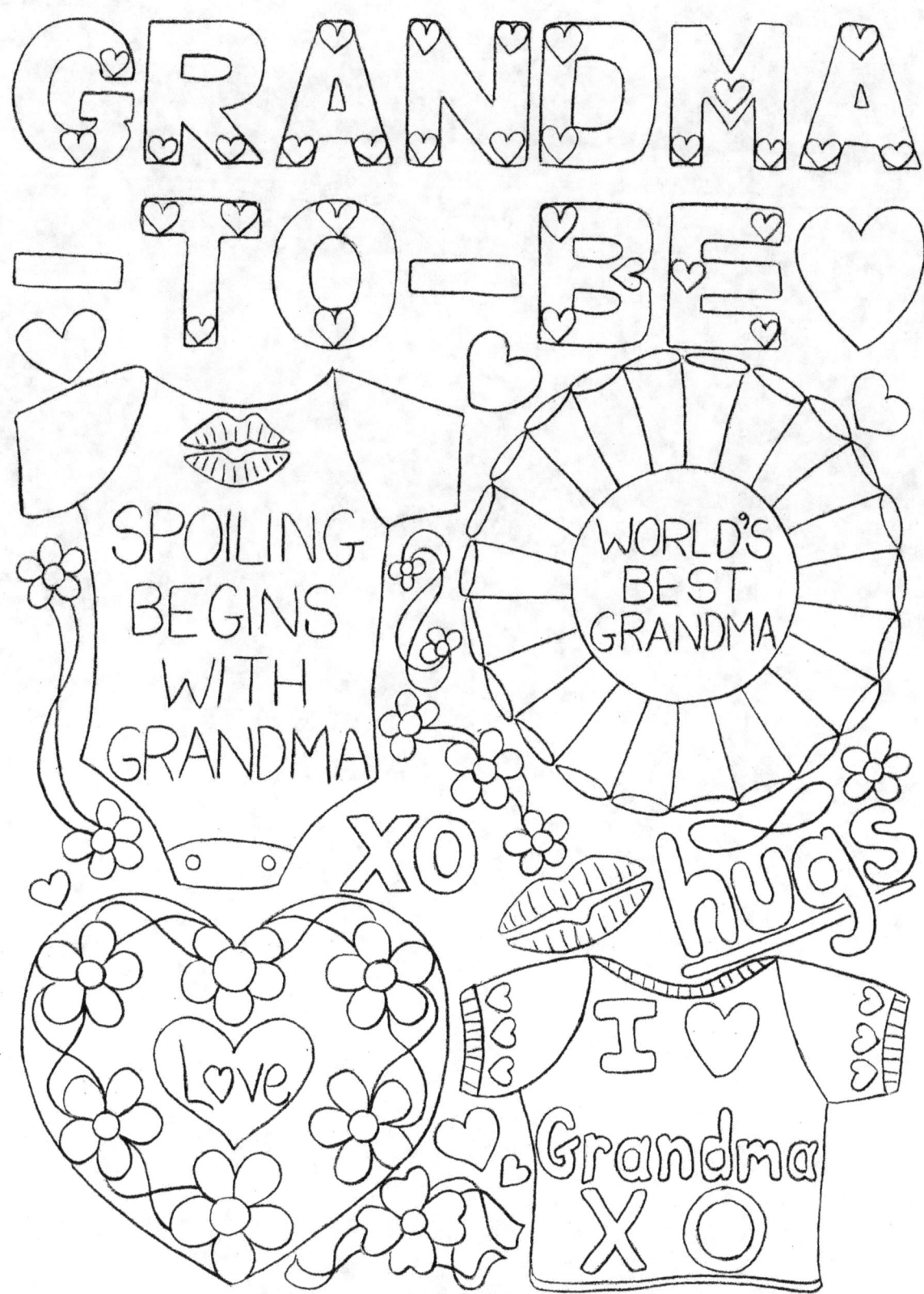

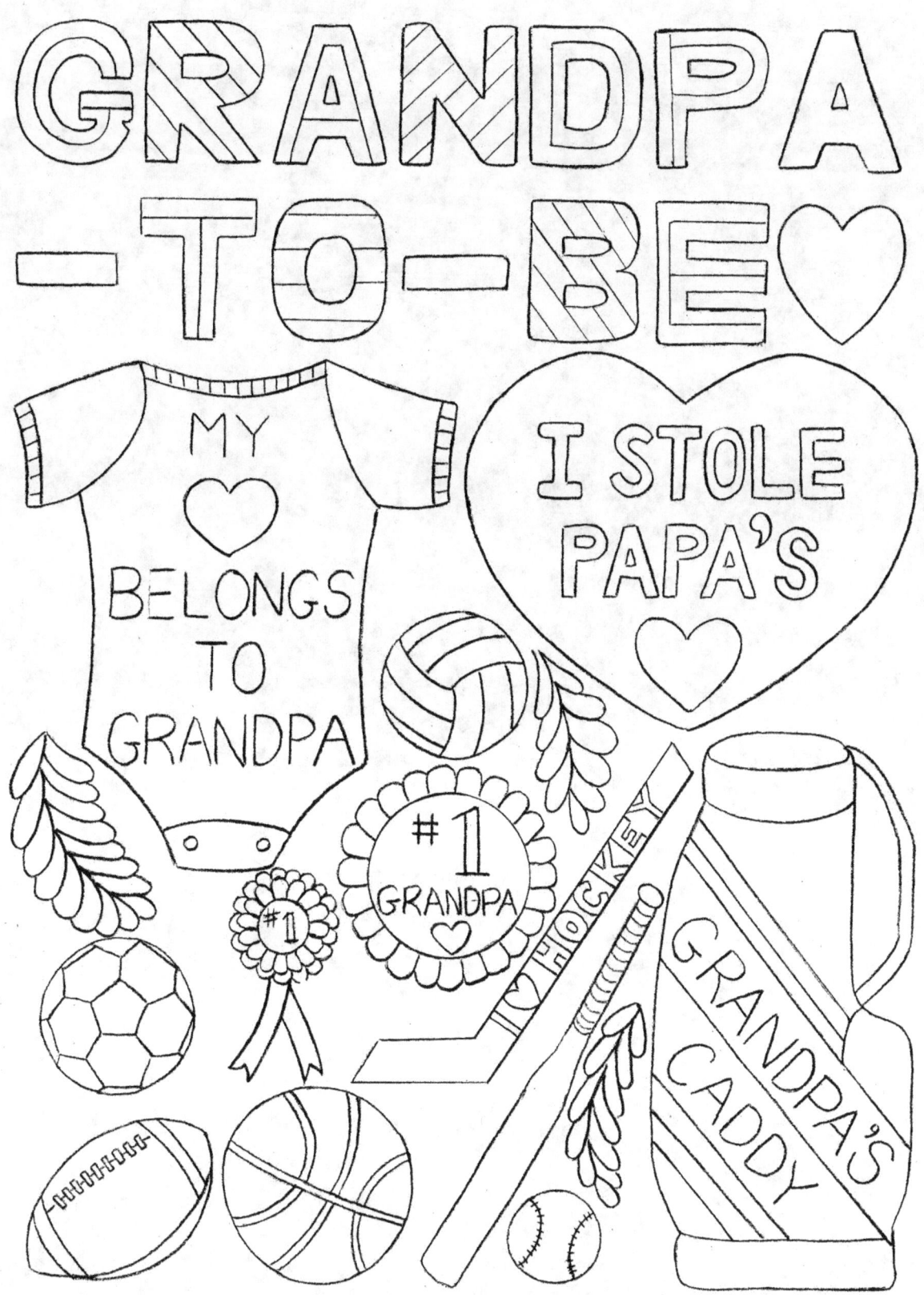

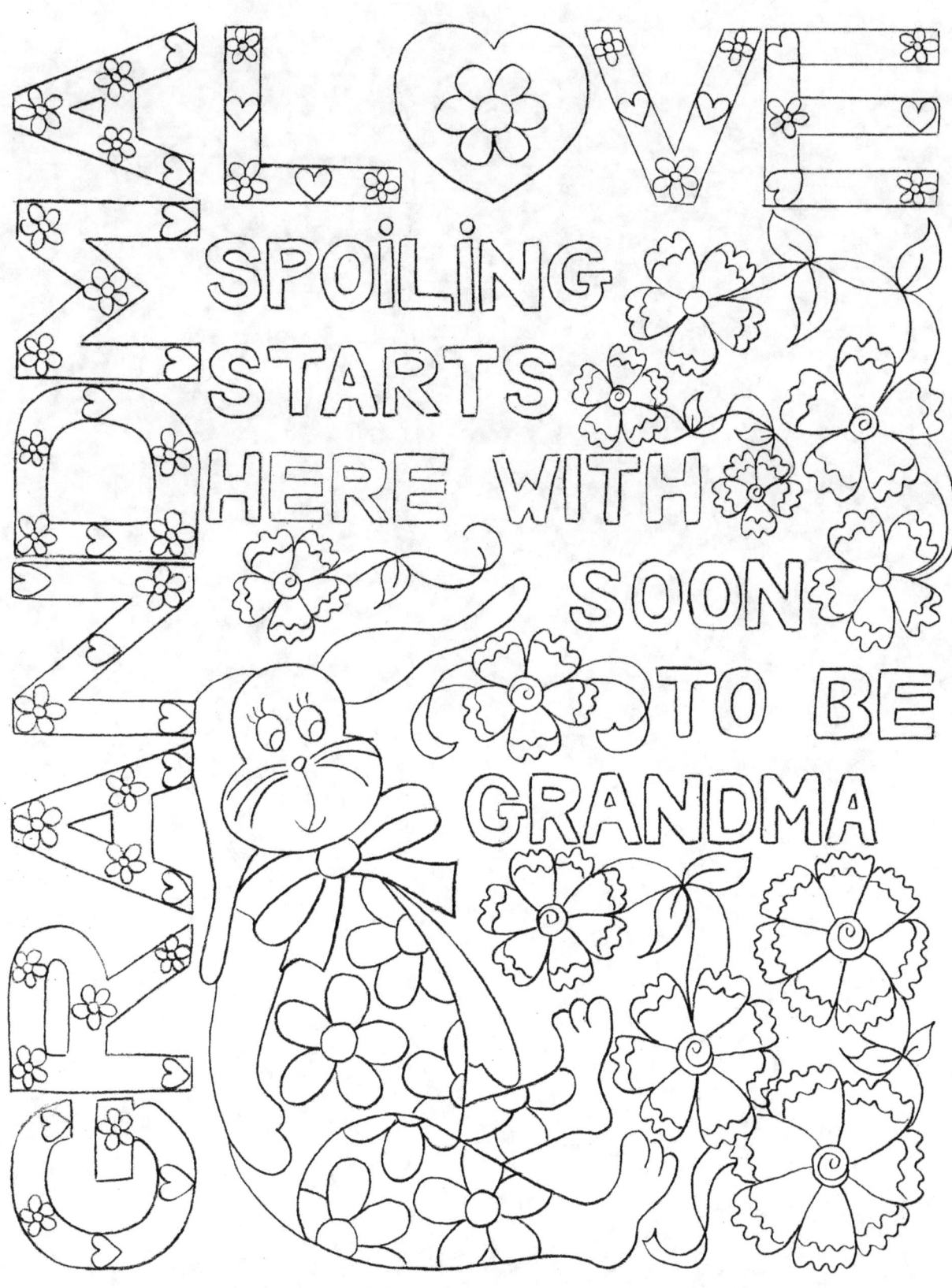

GRANDMA LOVE SPOILING STARTS HERE WITH SOON TO BE GRANDMA

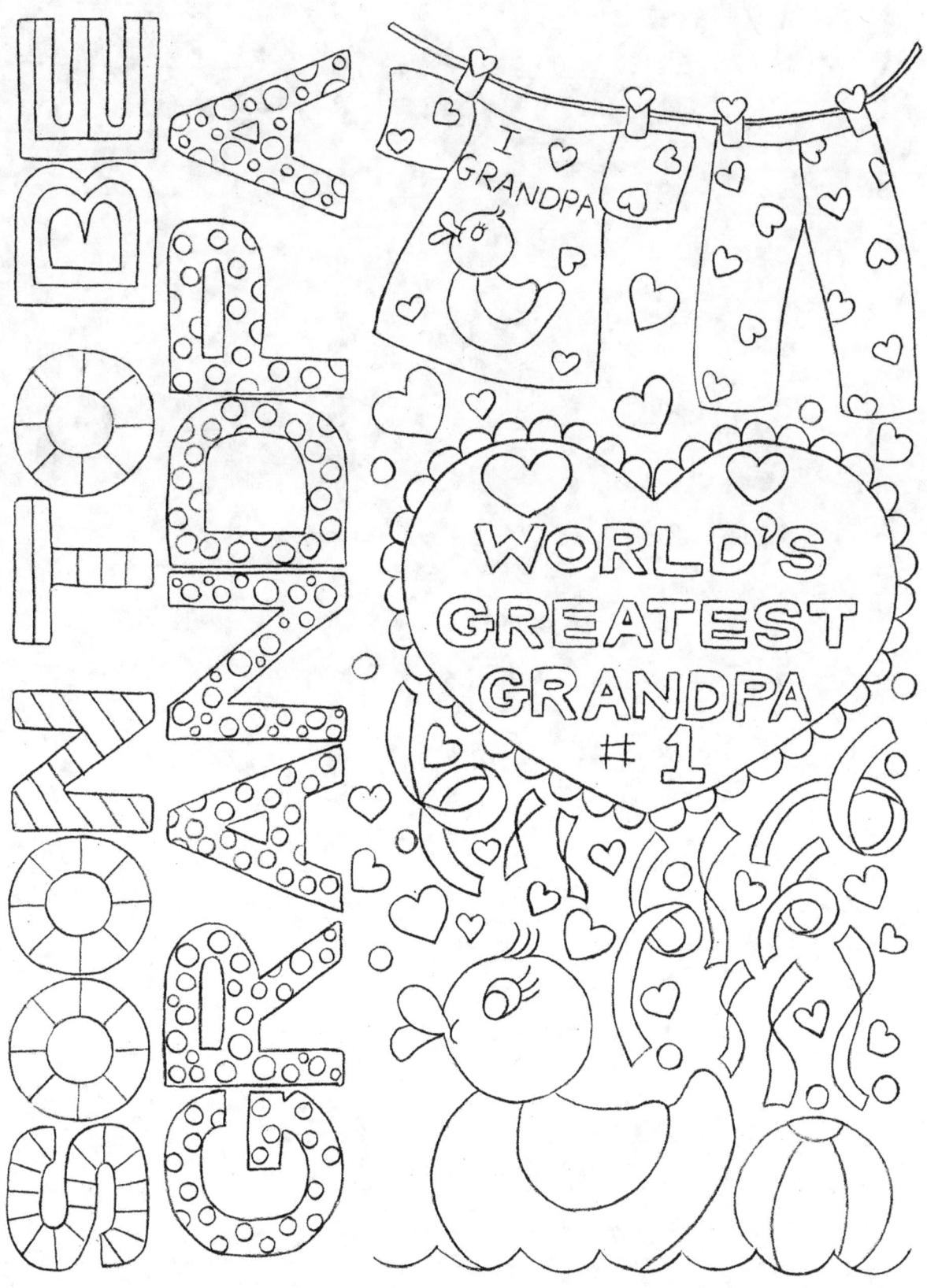

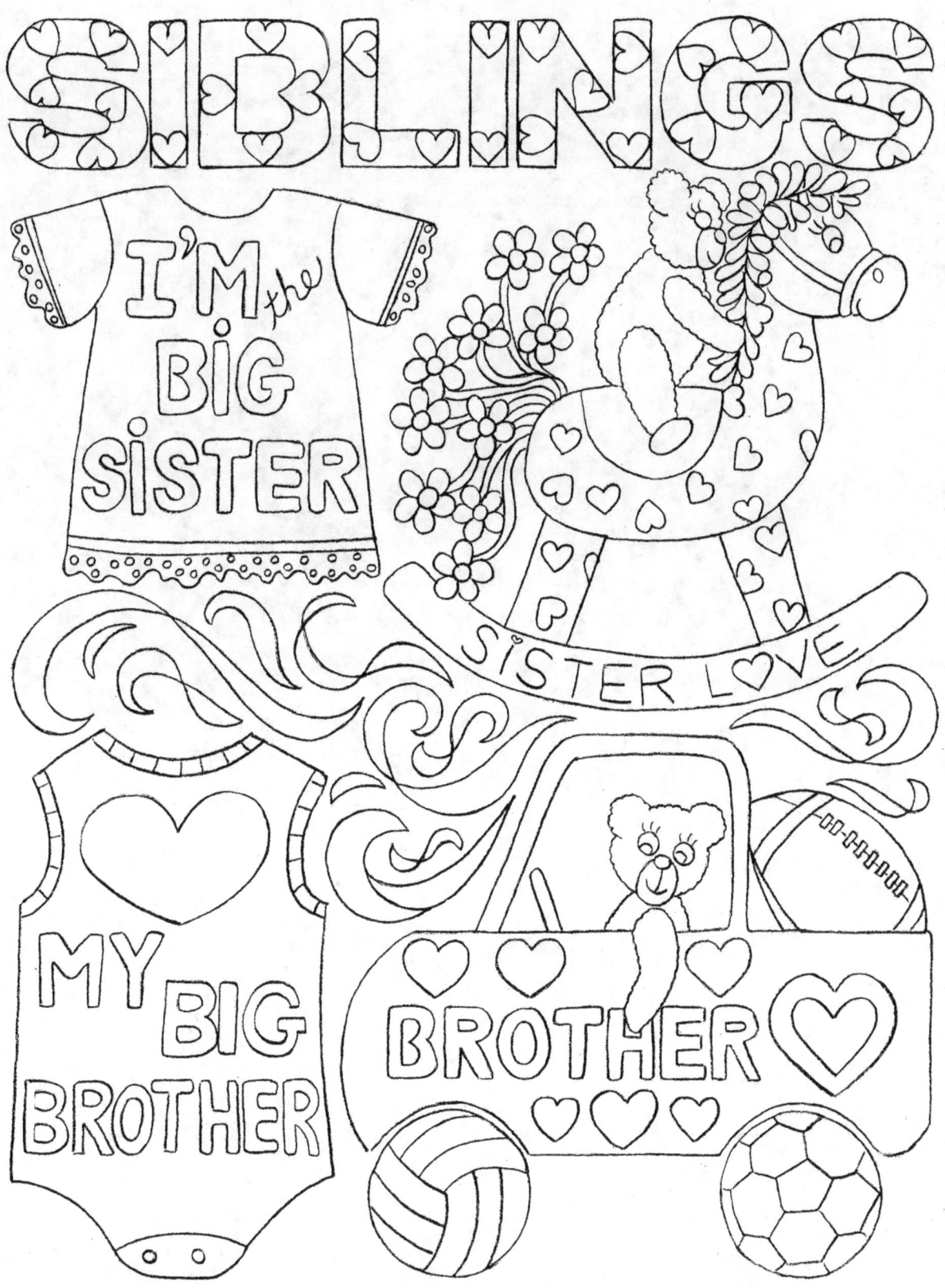

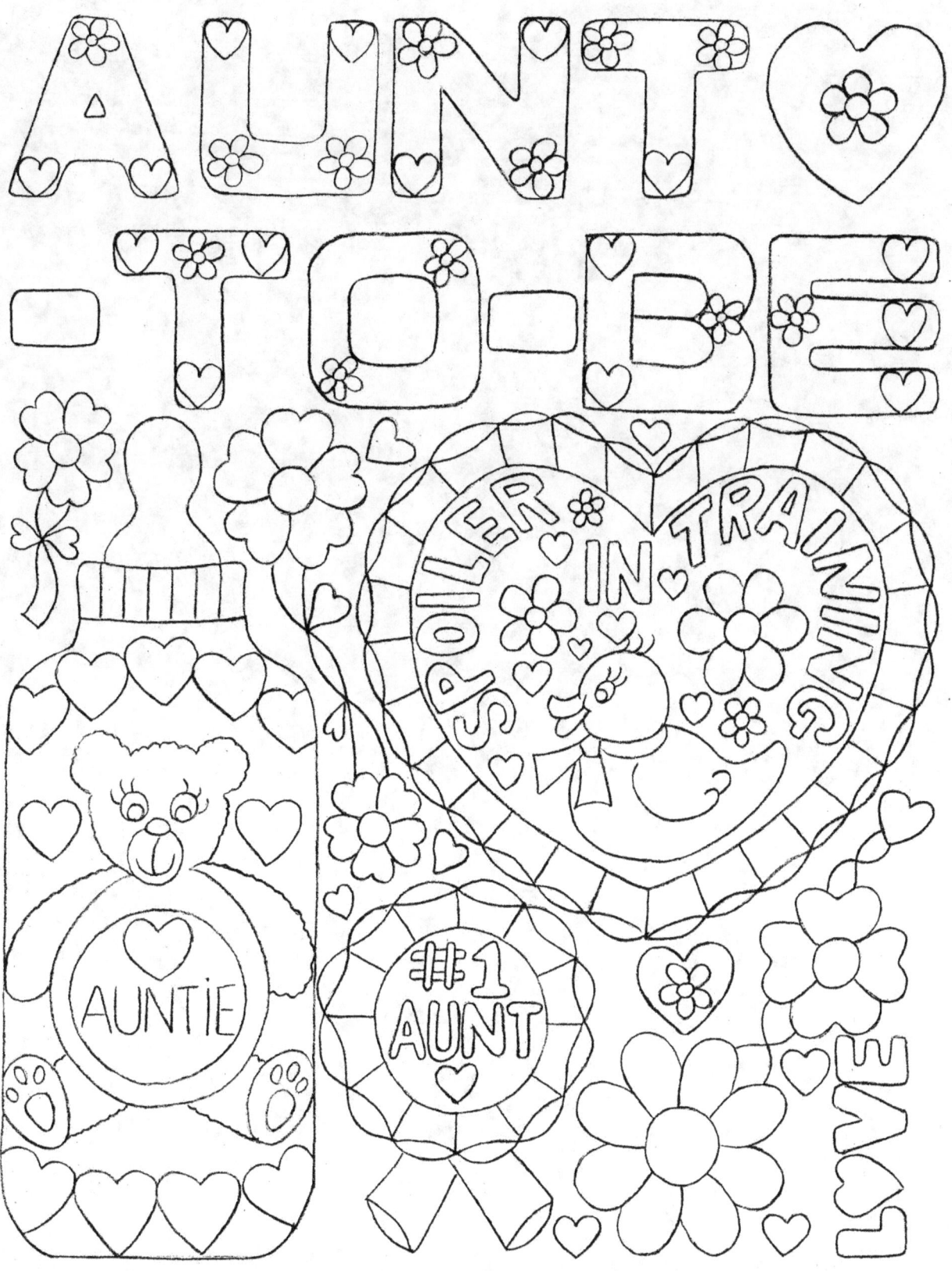

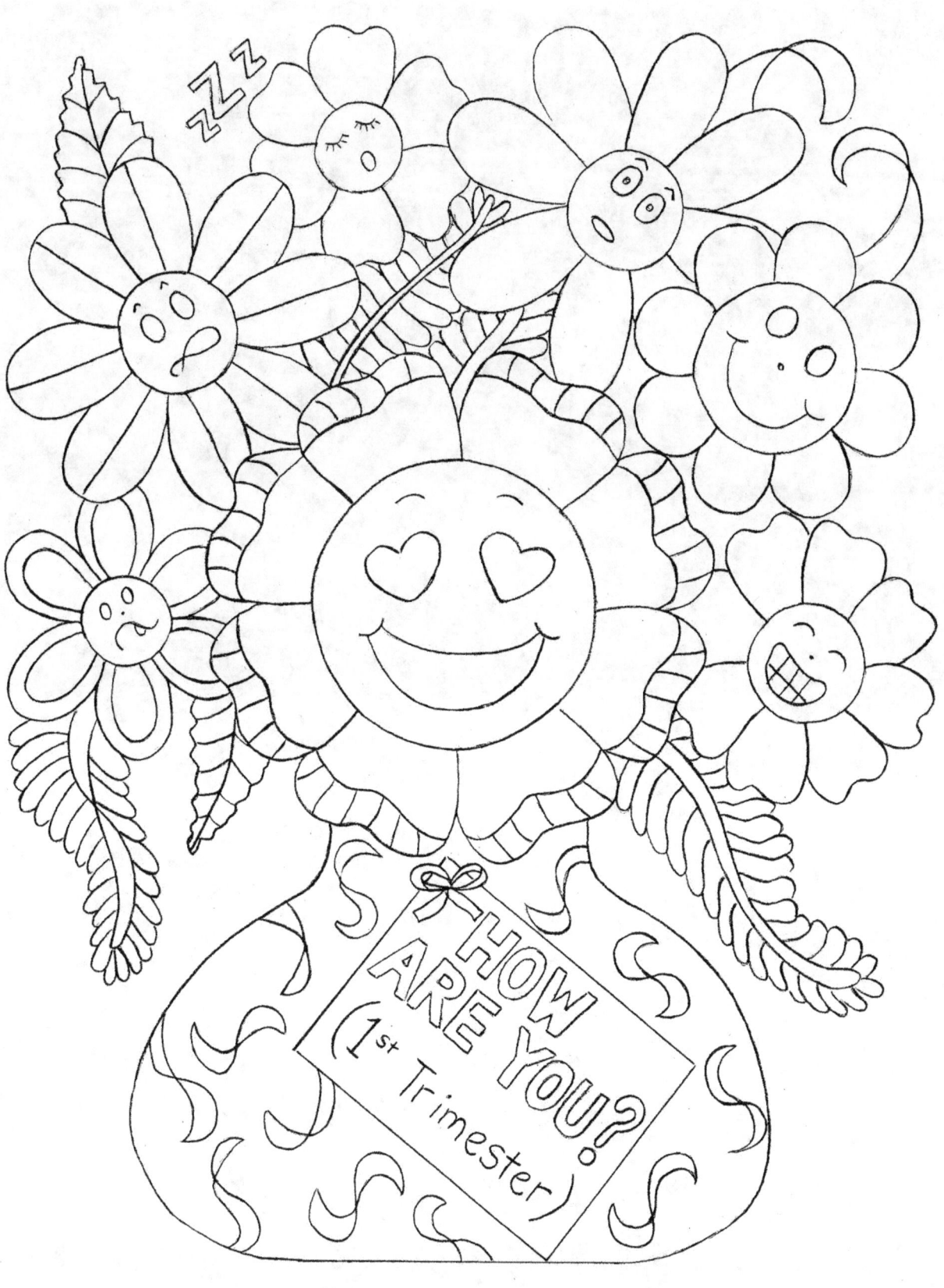

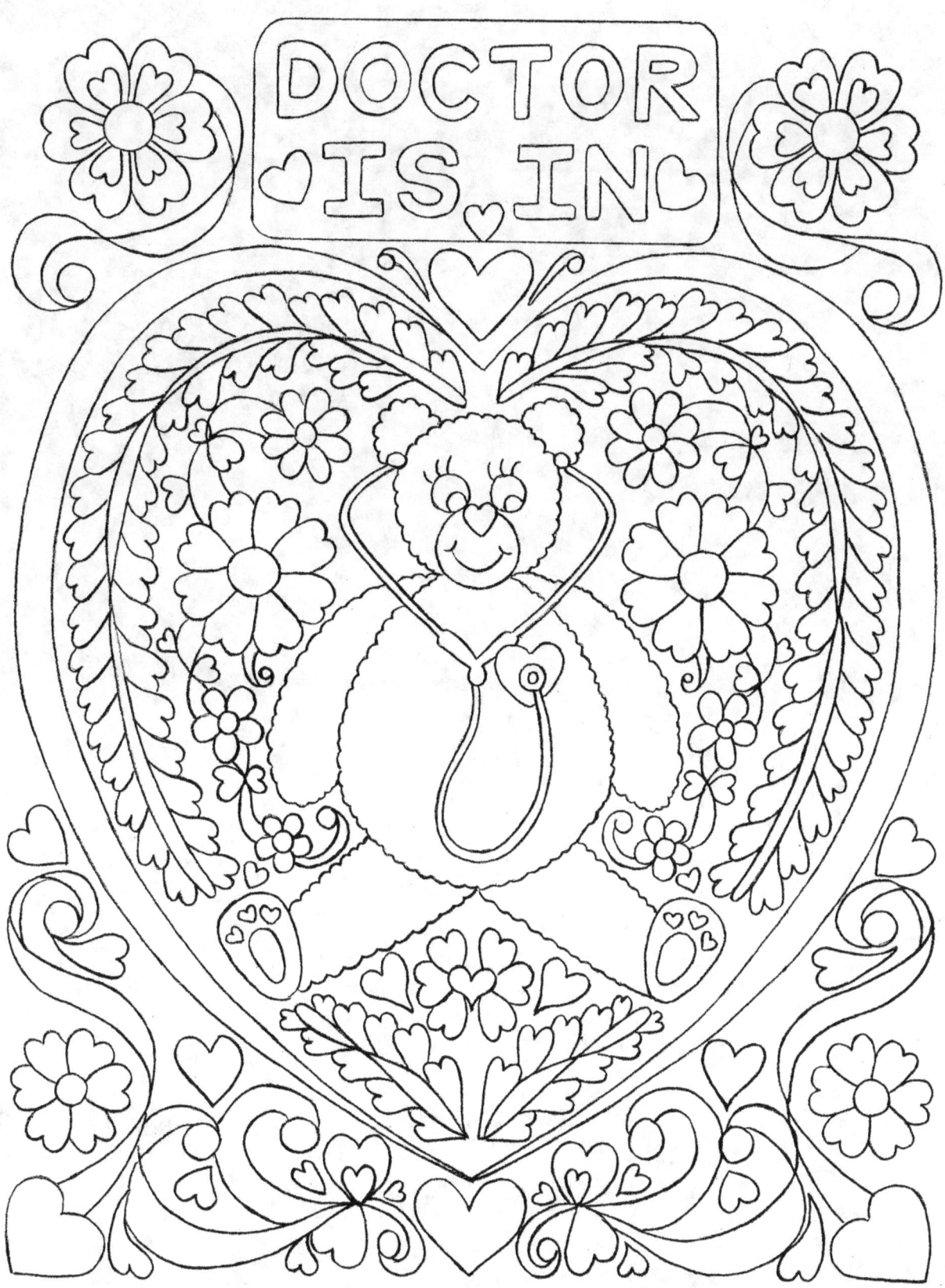

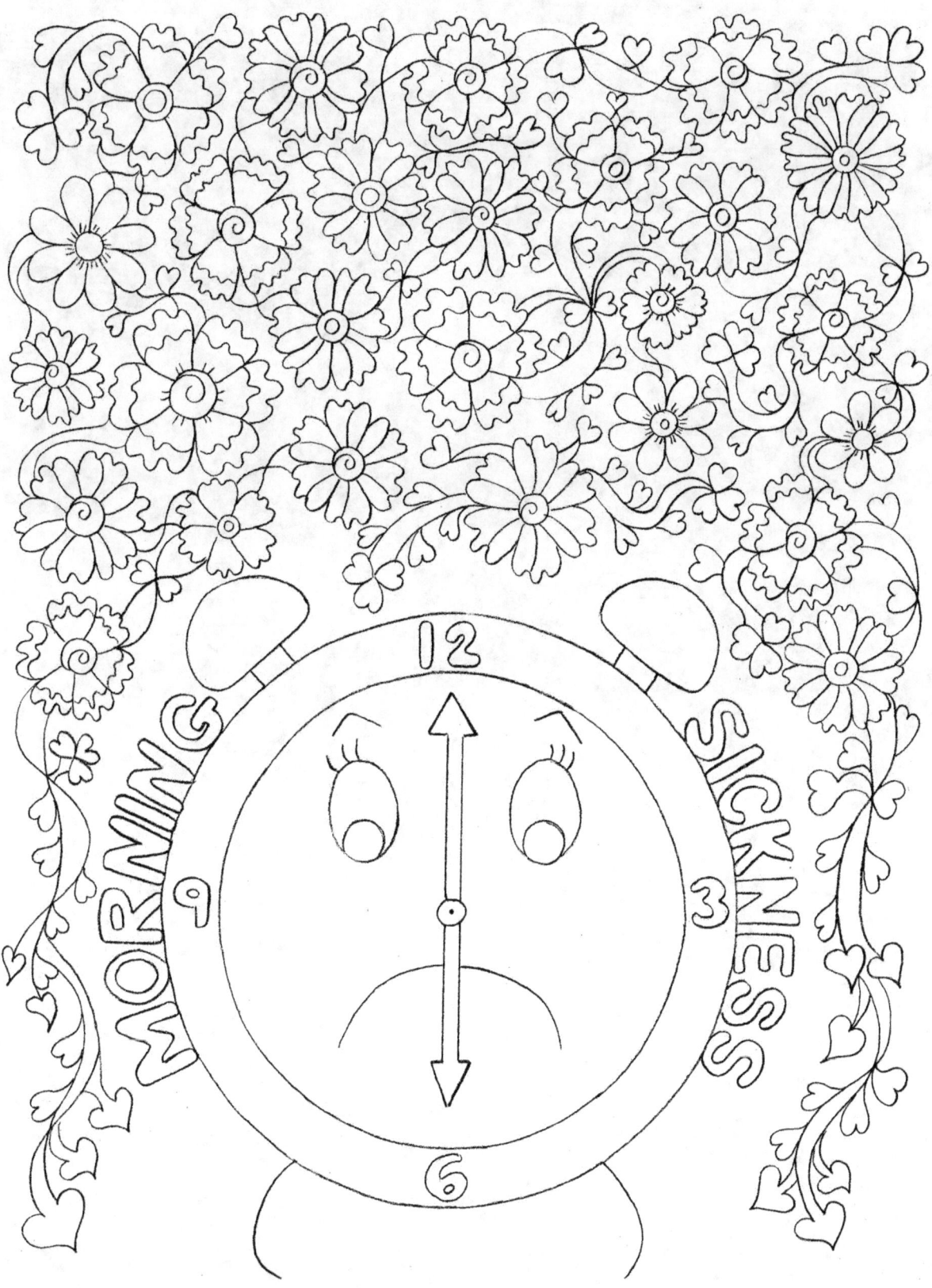

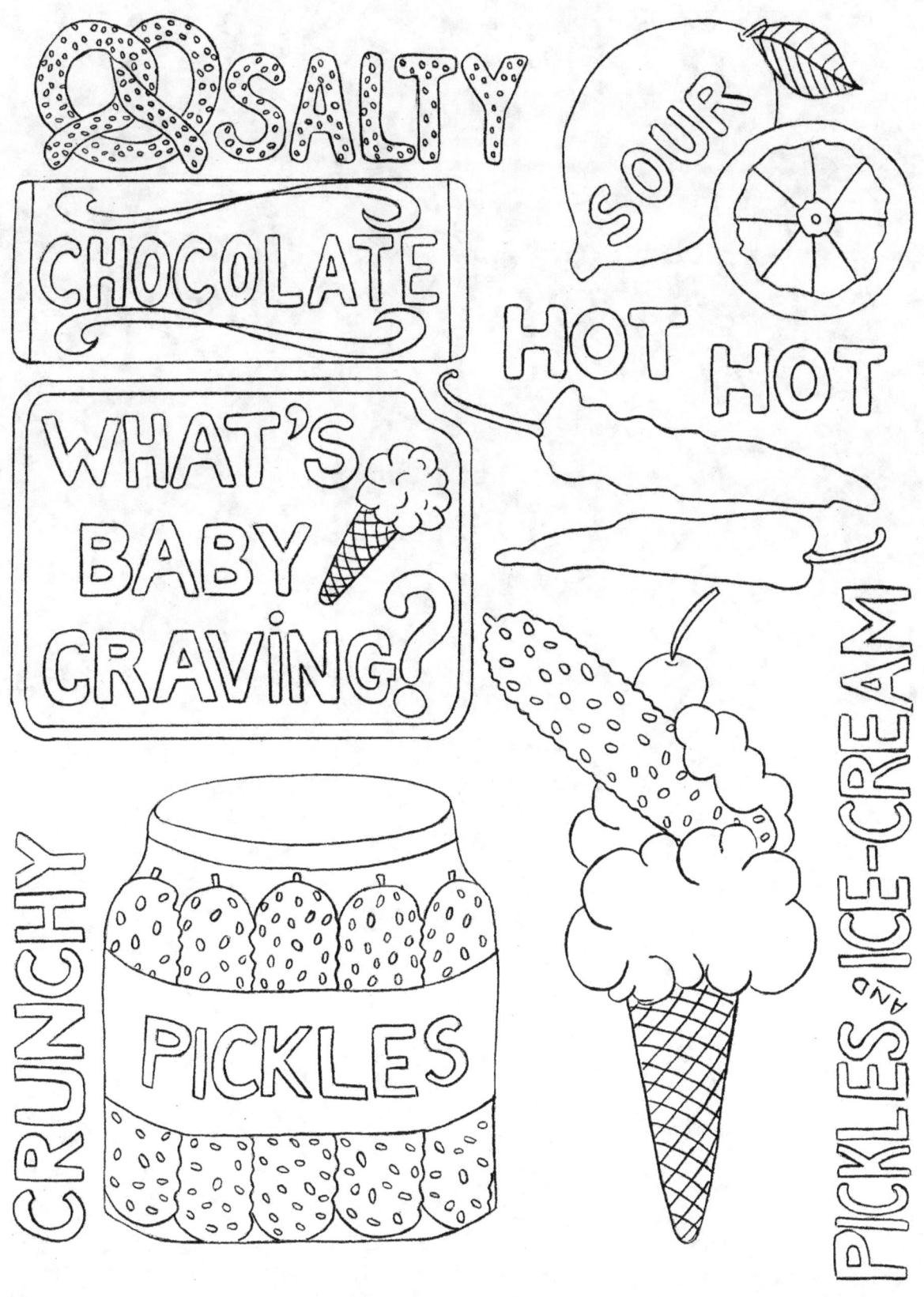

SALTY

CHOCOLATE

SOUR

HOT HOT HOT

WHAT'S BABY CRAVING?

CRUNCHY

PICKLES

PICKLES AND ICE-CREAM

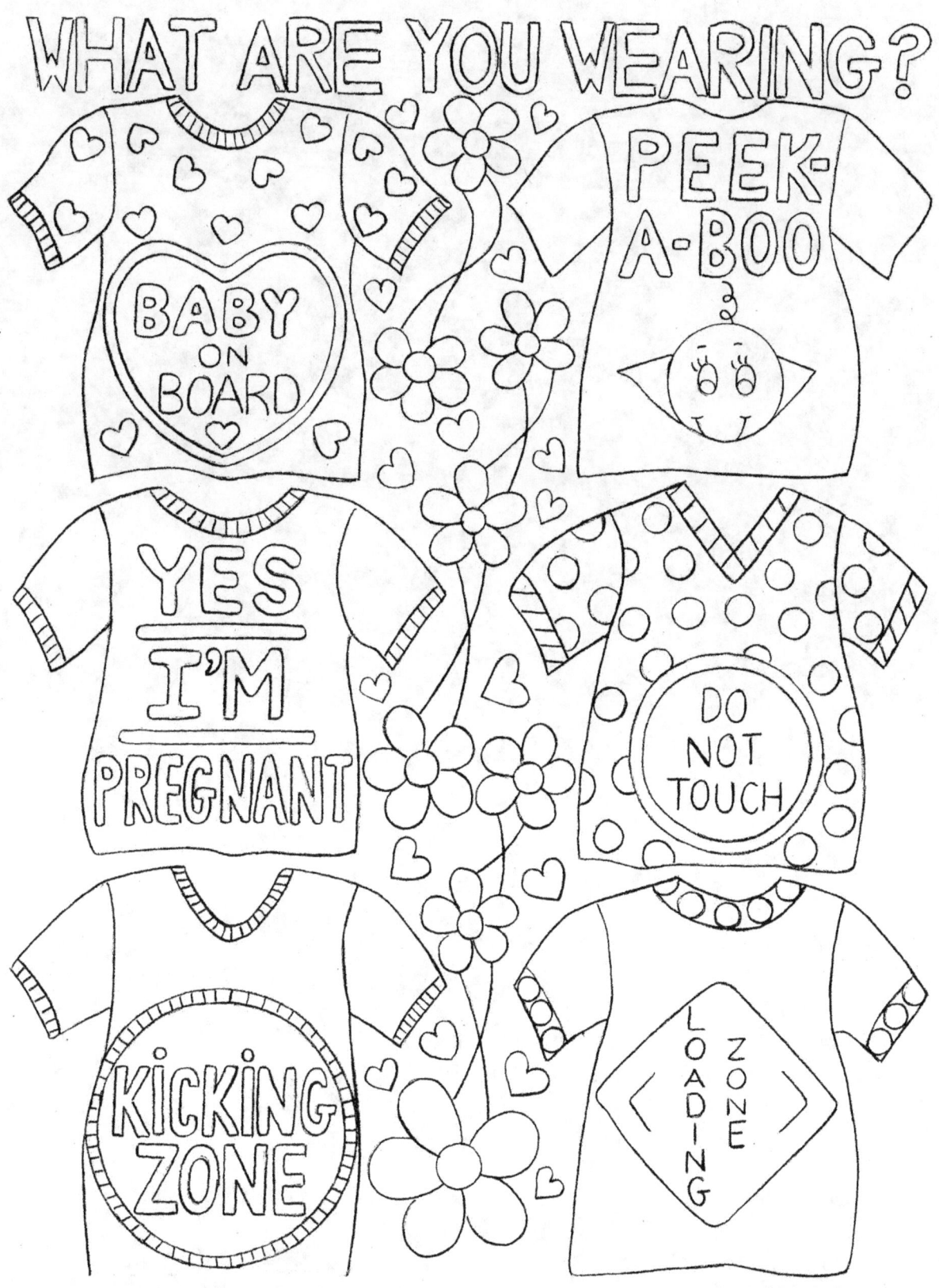

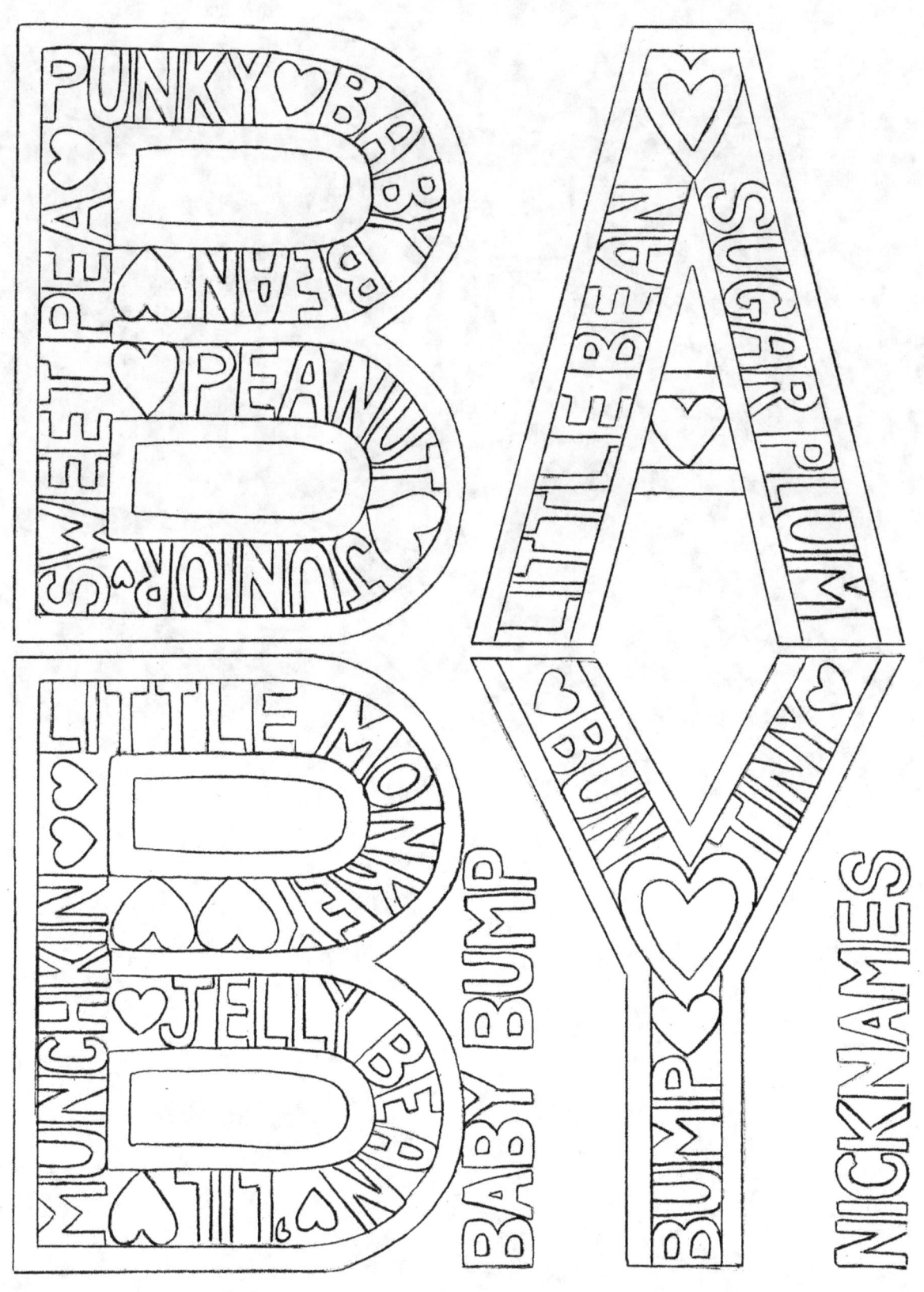

BABY

PUNKY BABY BEAN SWEET PEA PEANUT JUNIOR LITTLE MONKEY MUNCHKIN JELLY BEAN LITTLE BEAN SUGAR PLUM BUM TINY BUMP BABY BUMP

NICKNAMES

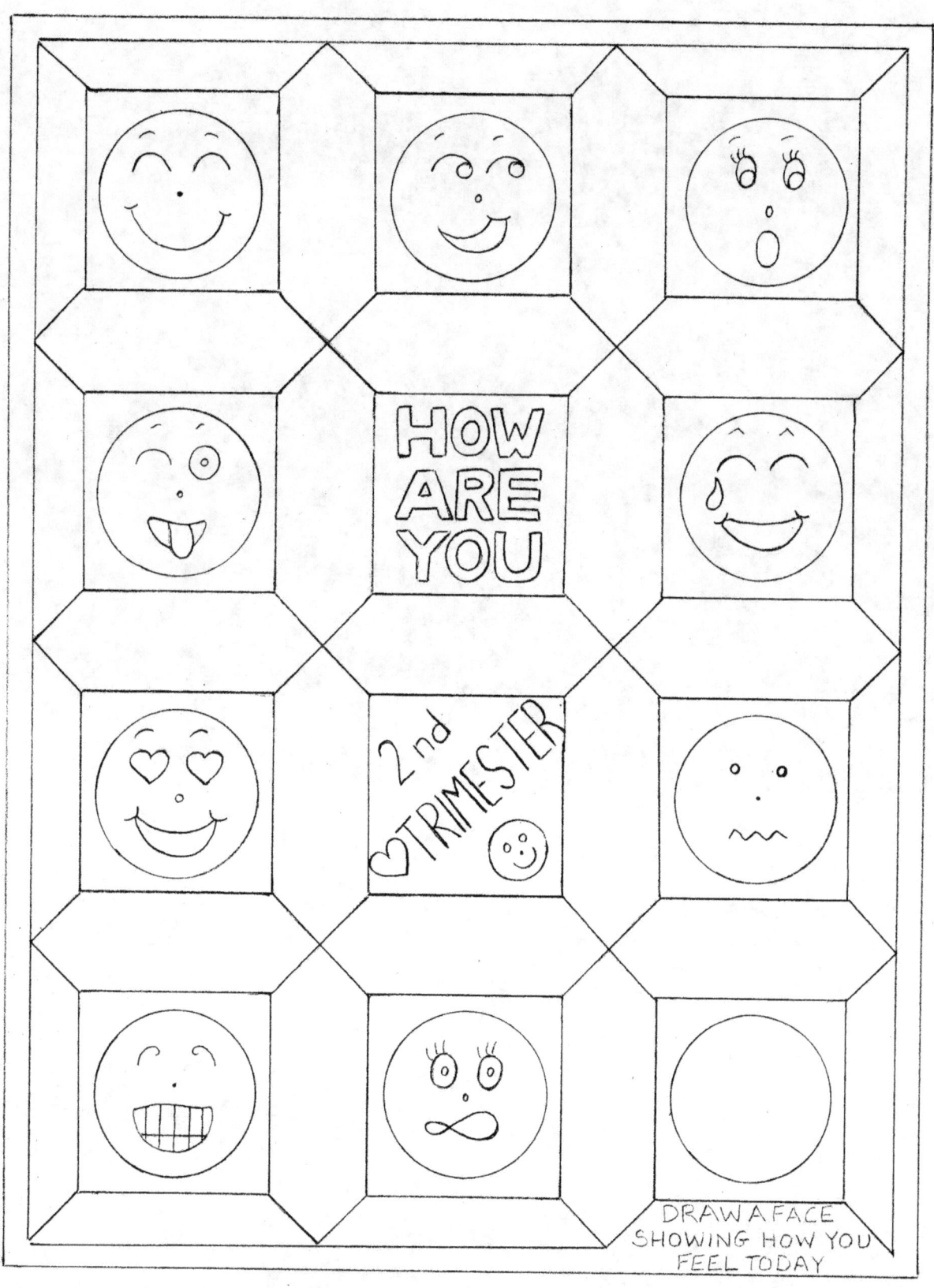

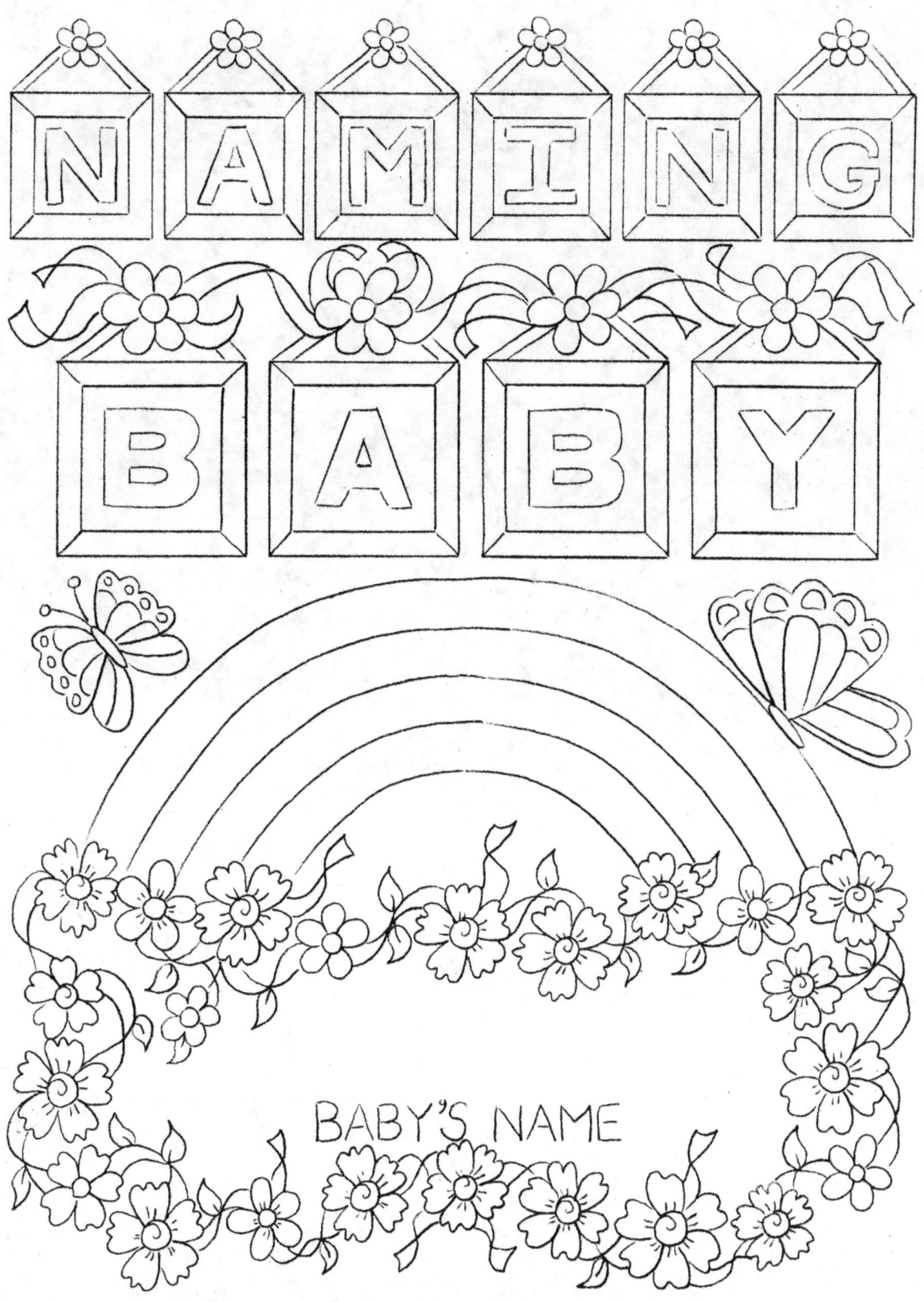

NAMING
BABY

BABY'S NAME

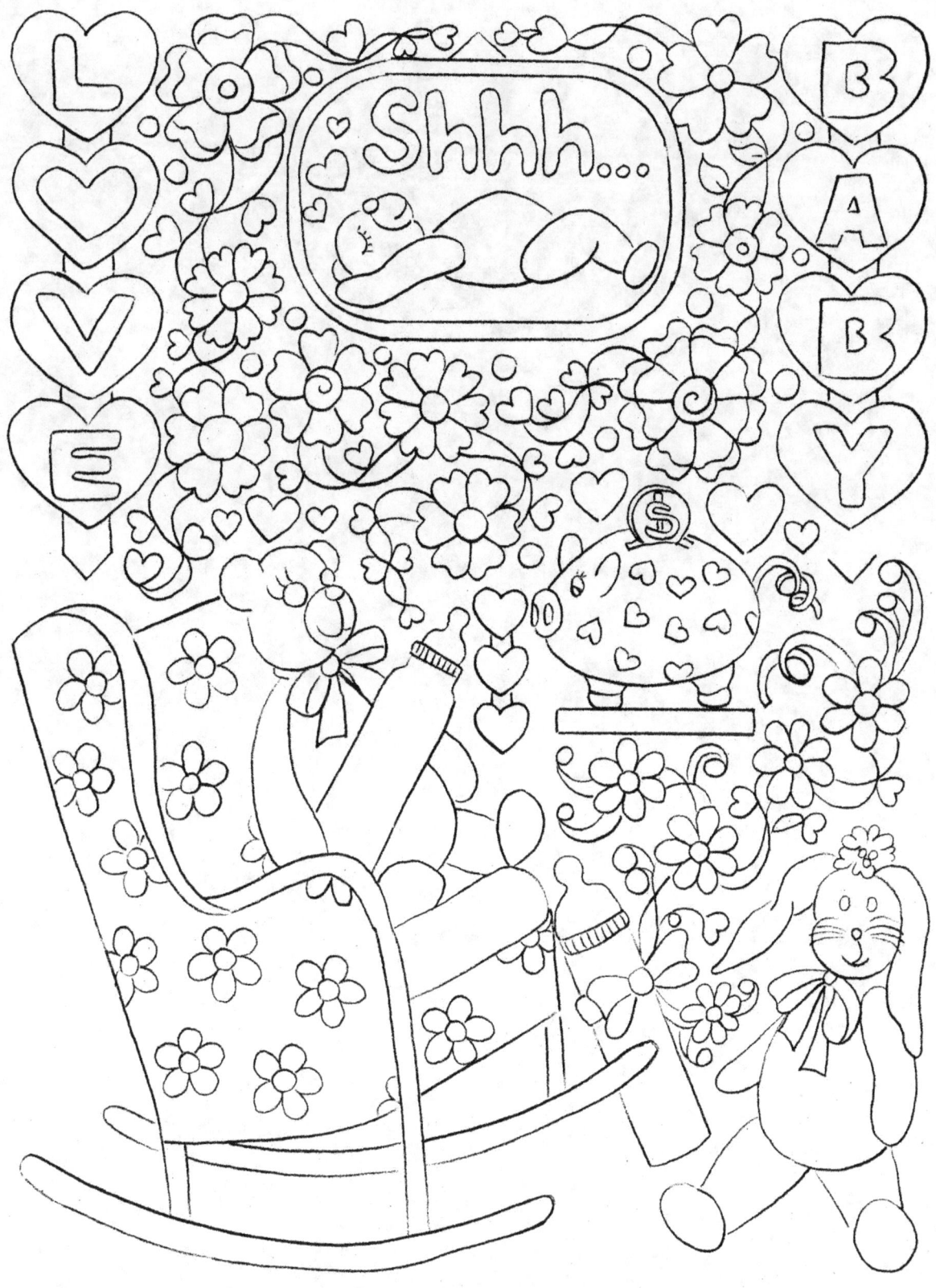

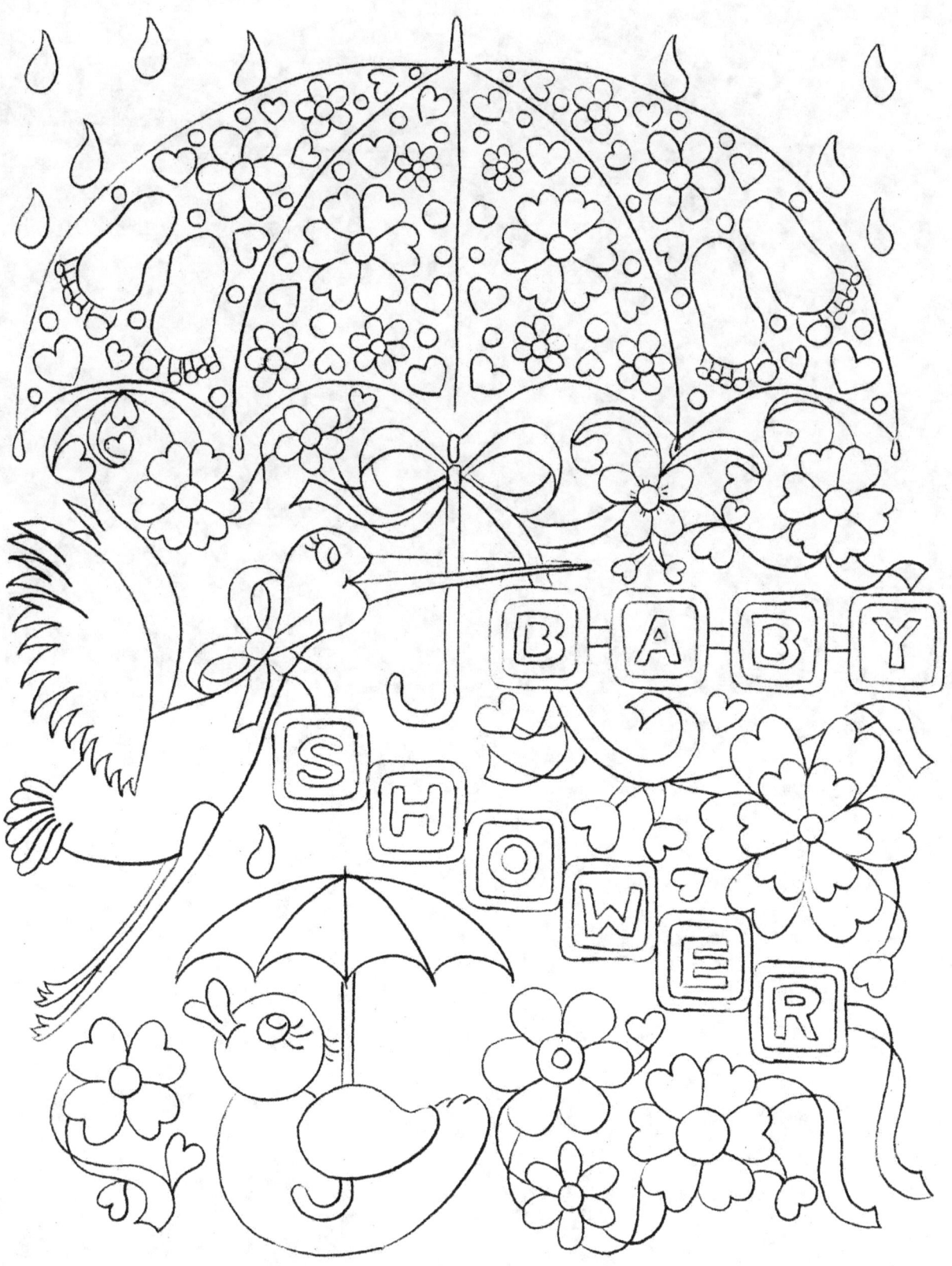

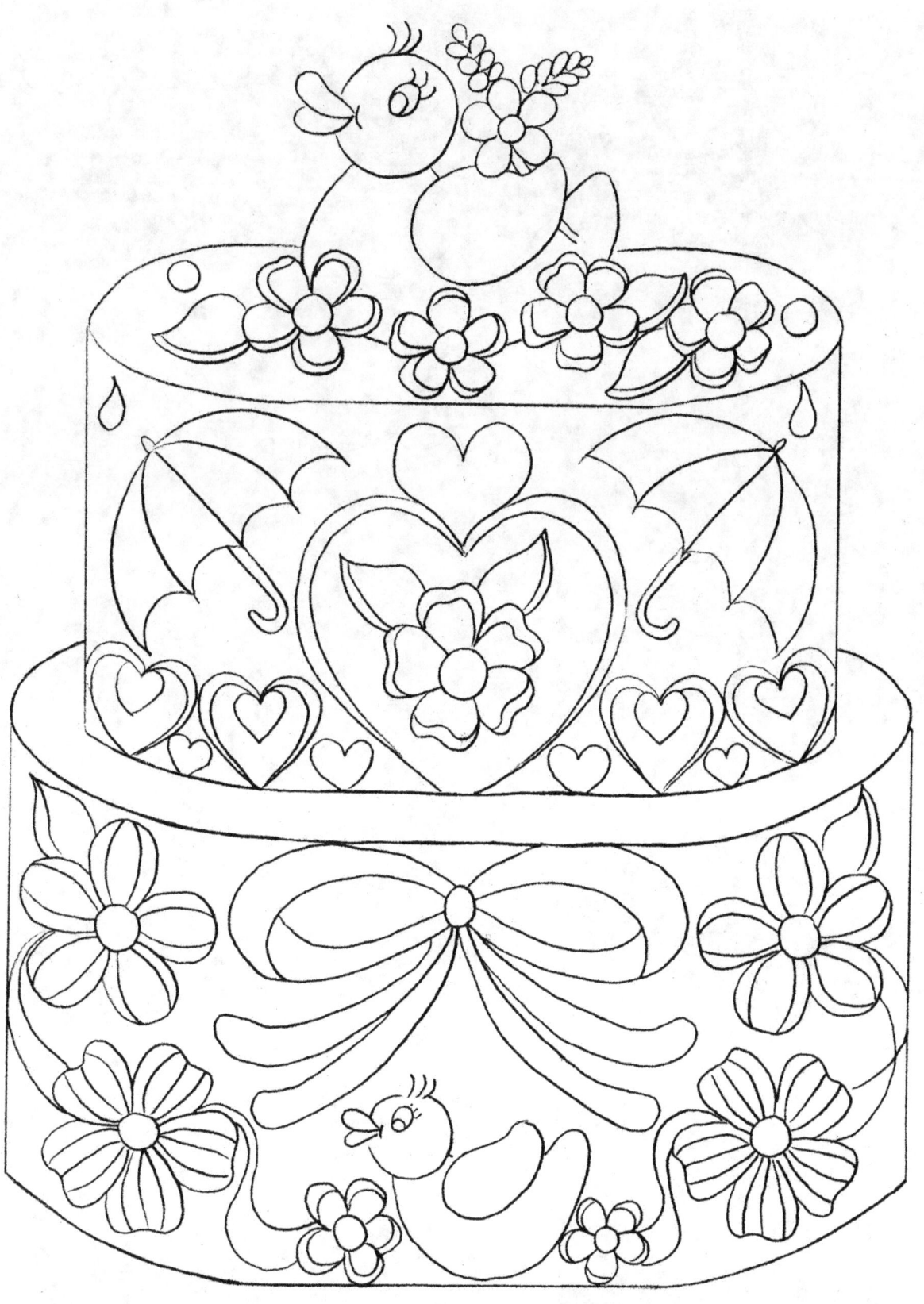

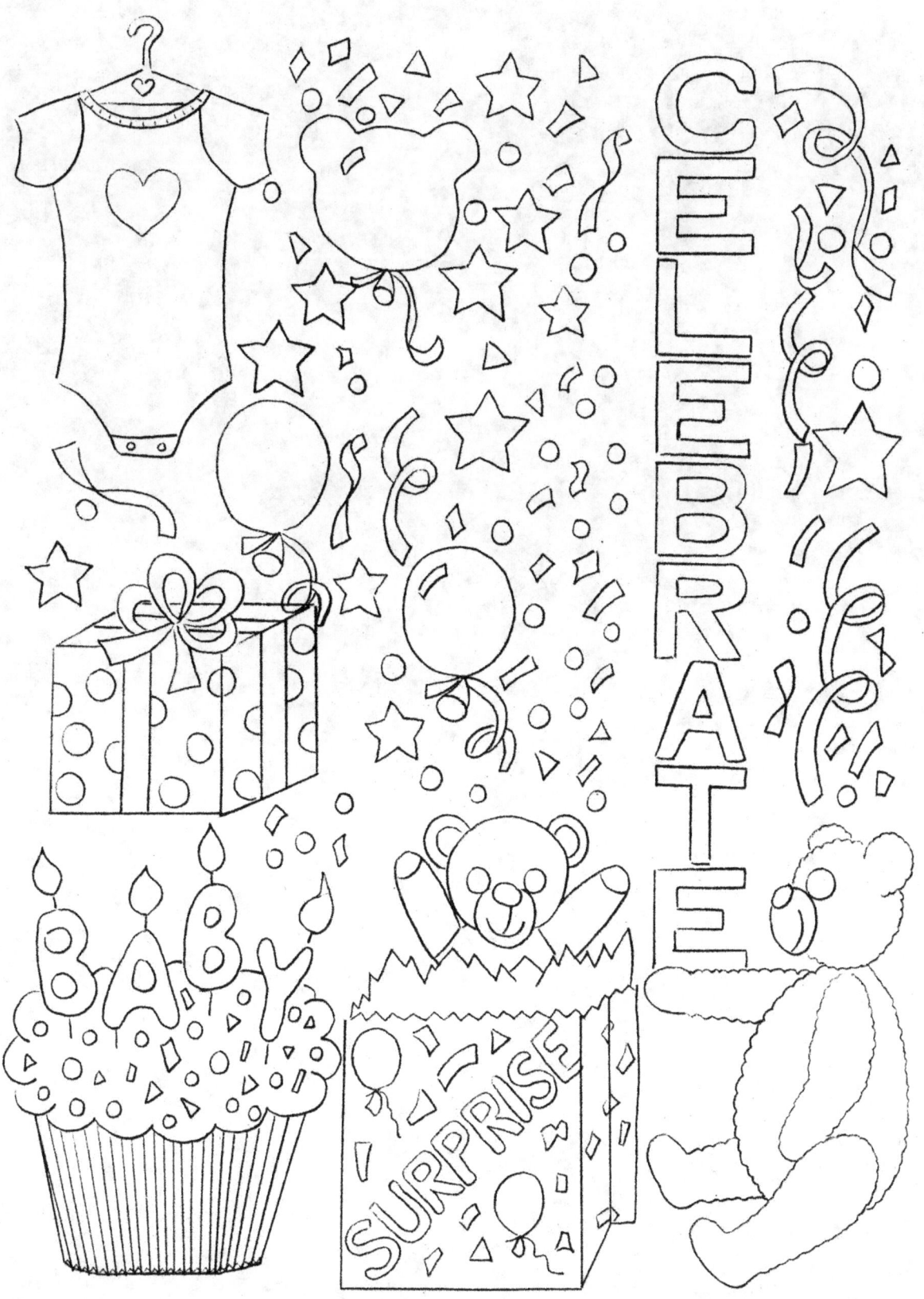

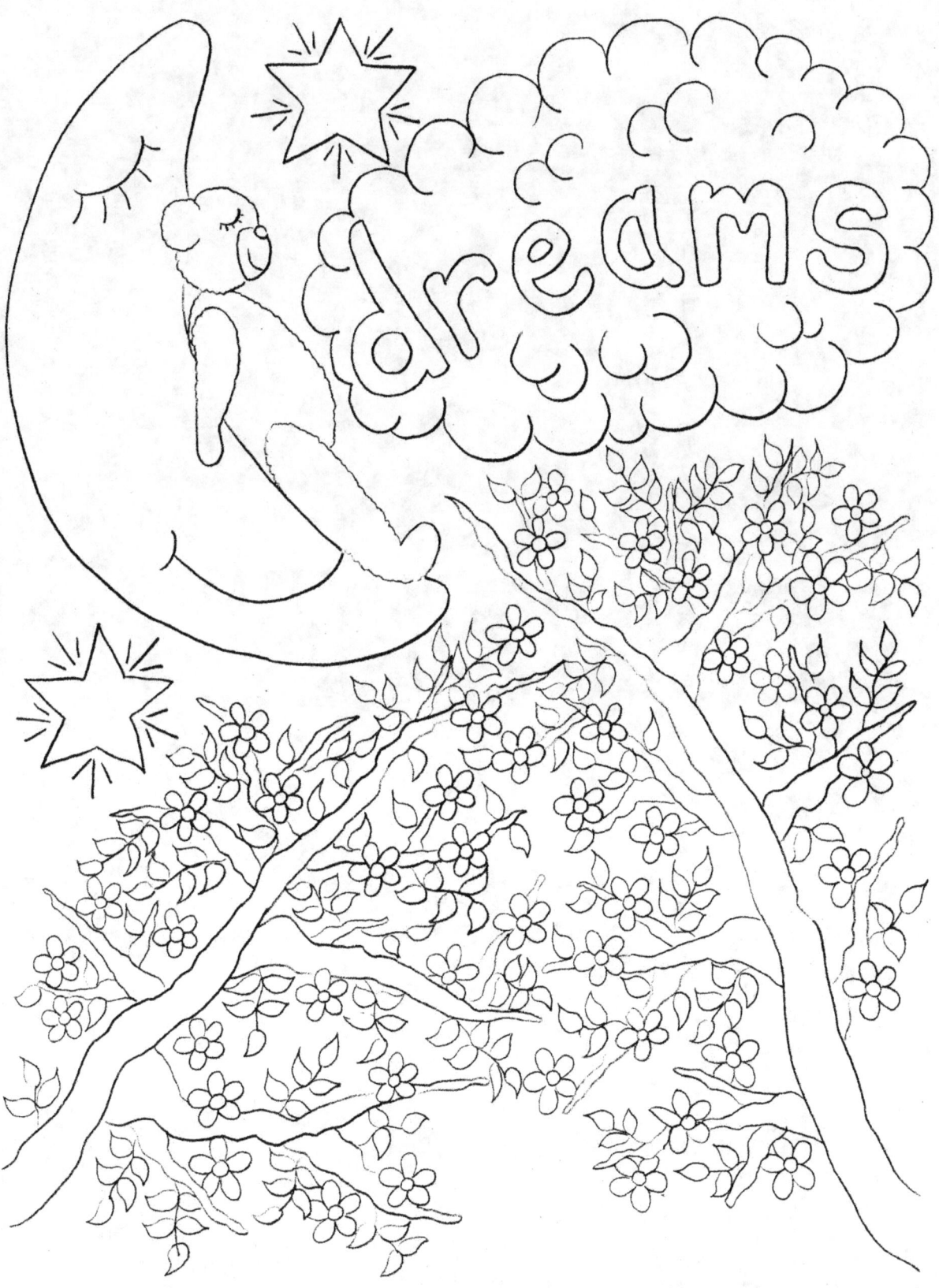

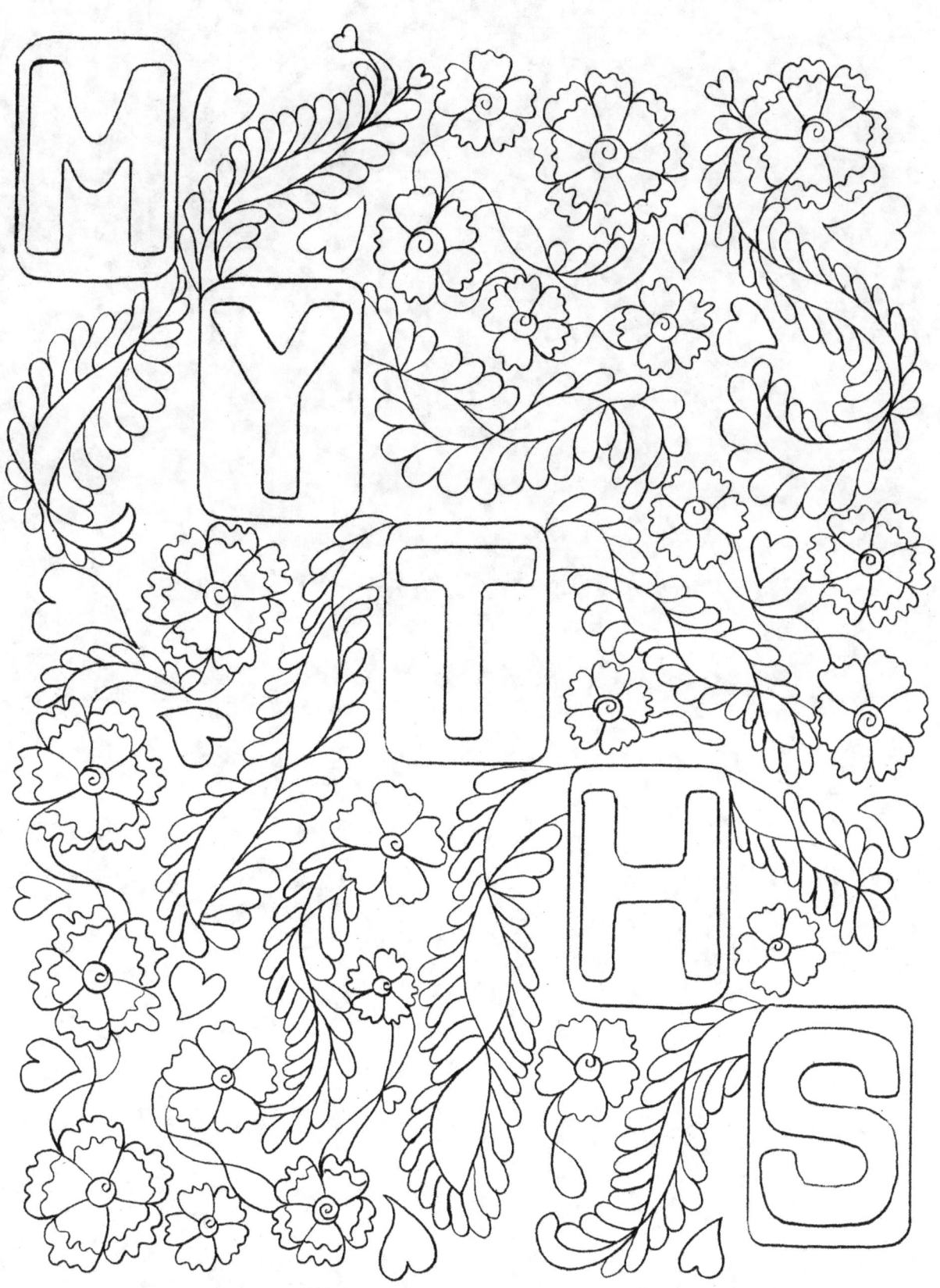

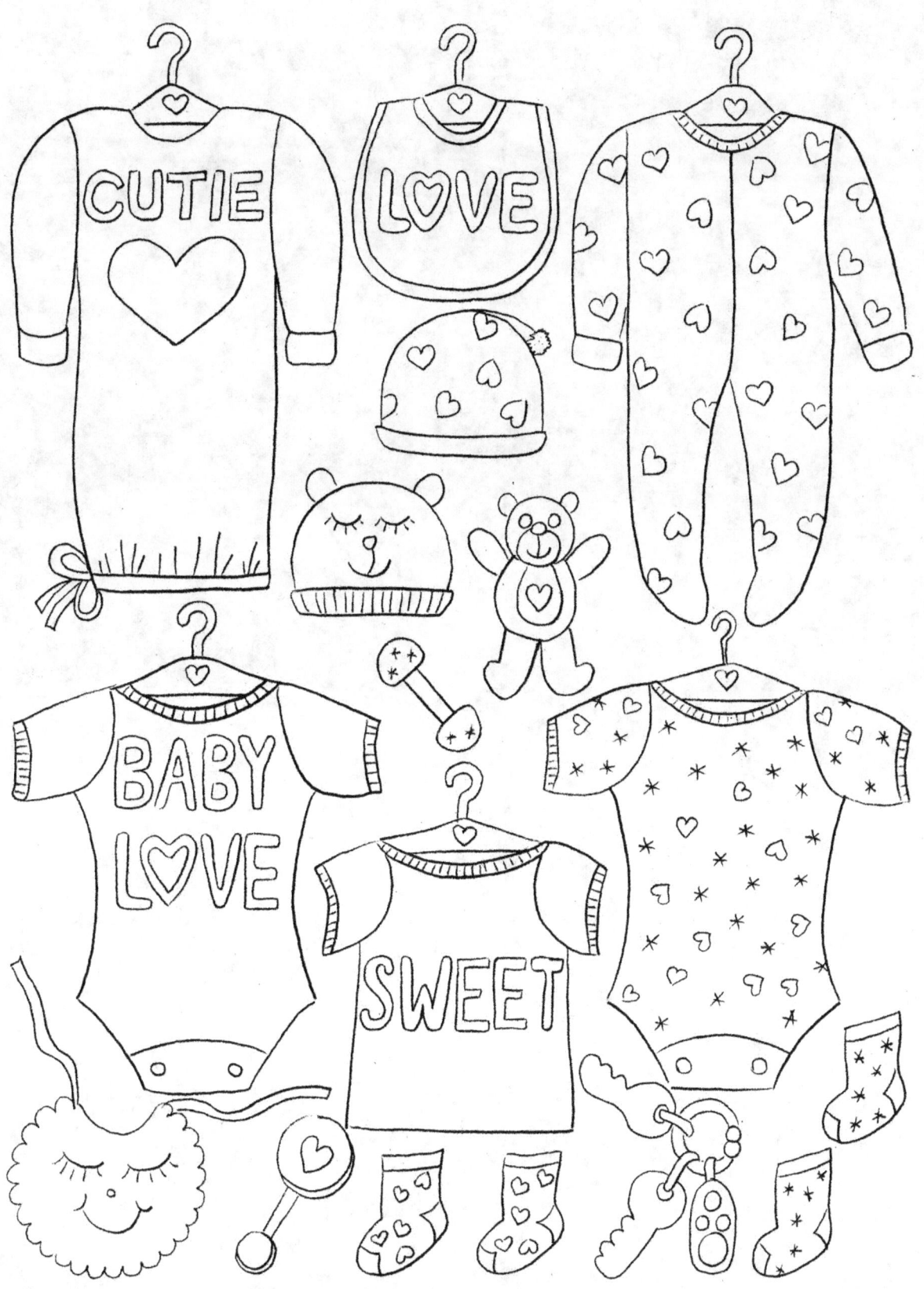

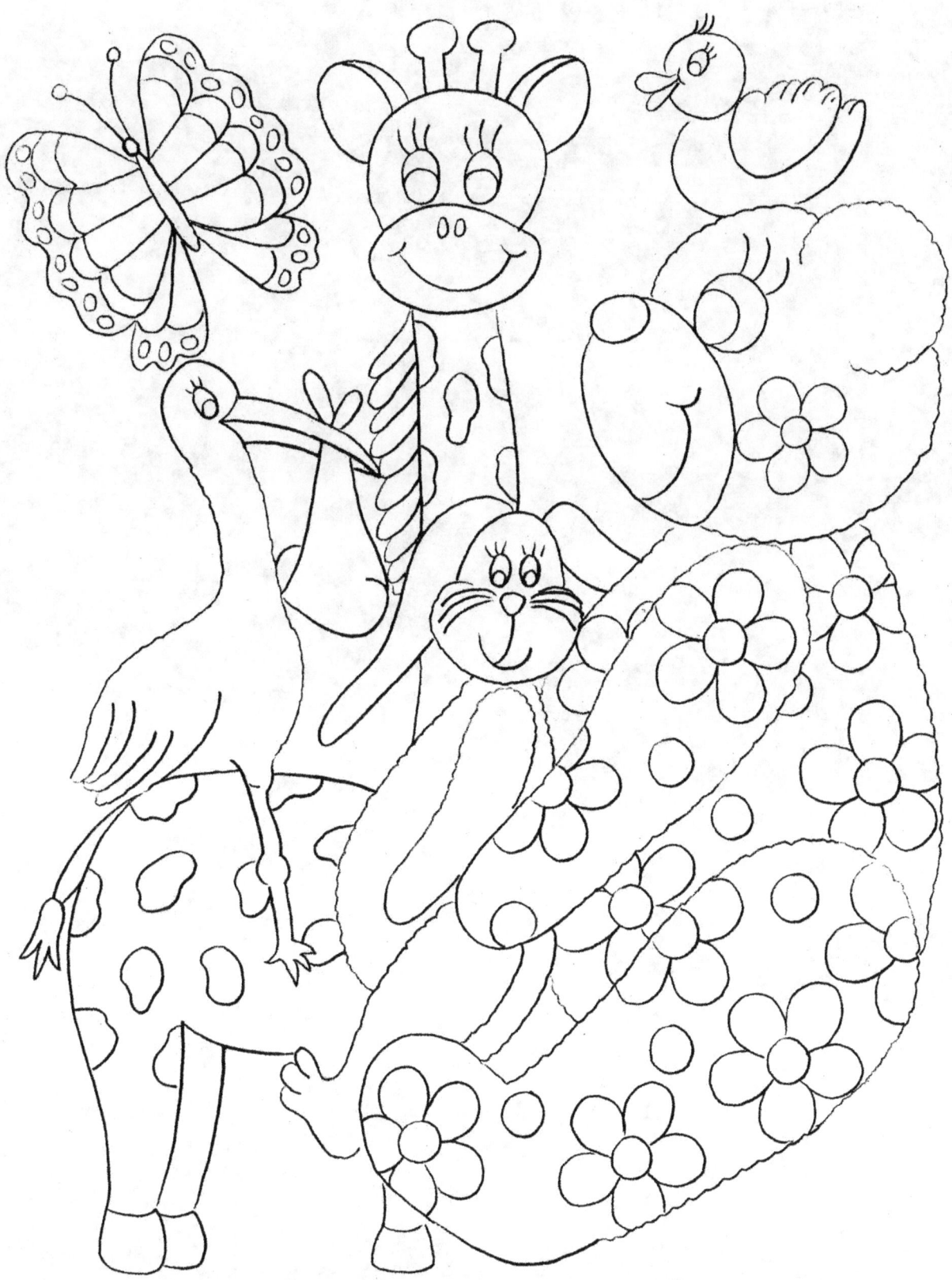

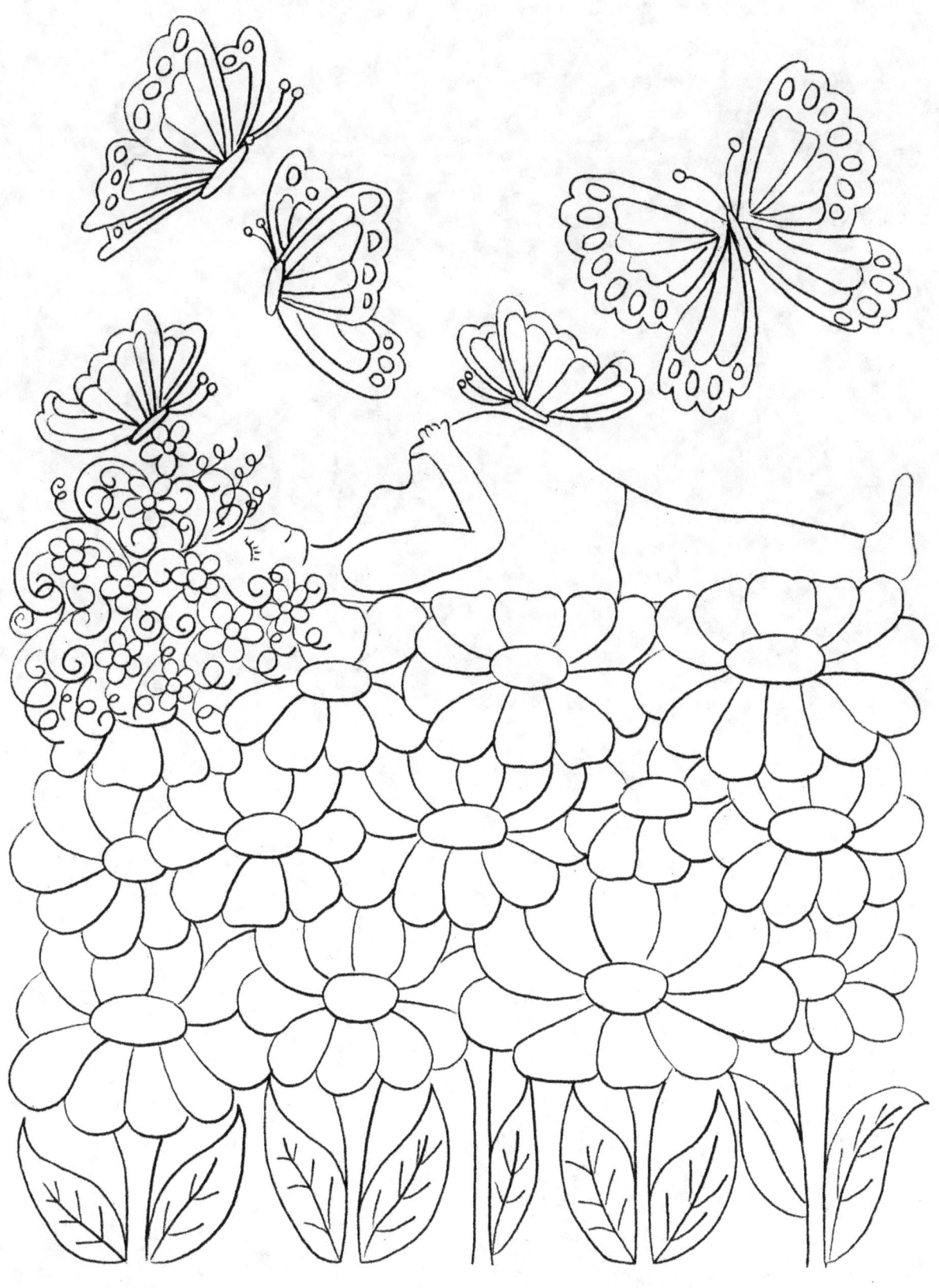

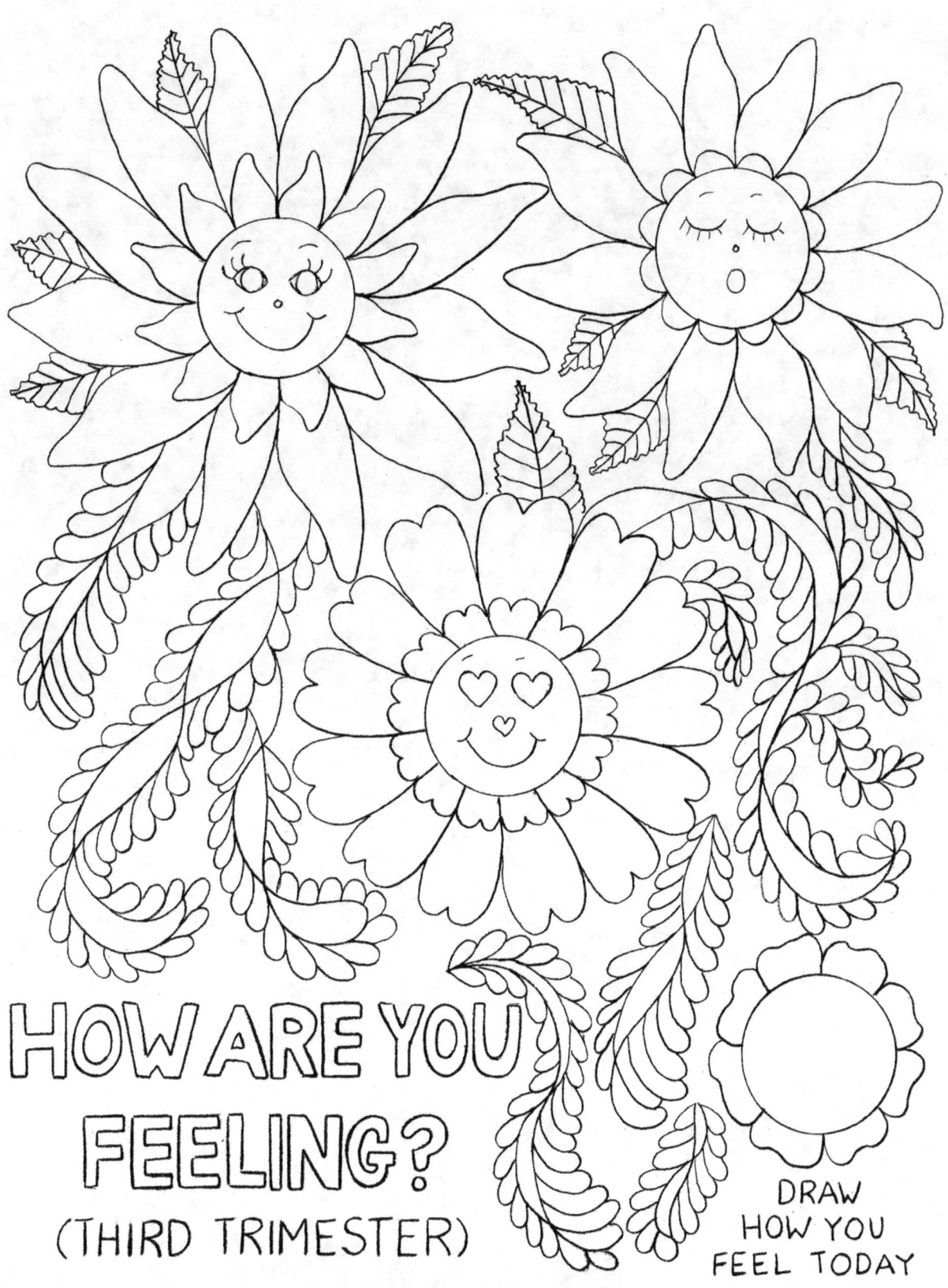

HOW ARE YOU FEELING?
(THIRD TRIMESTER)

DRAW HOW YOU FEEL TODAY

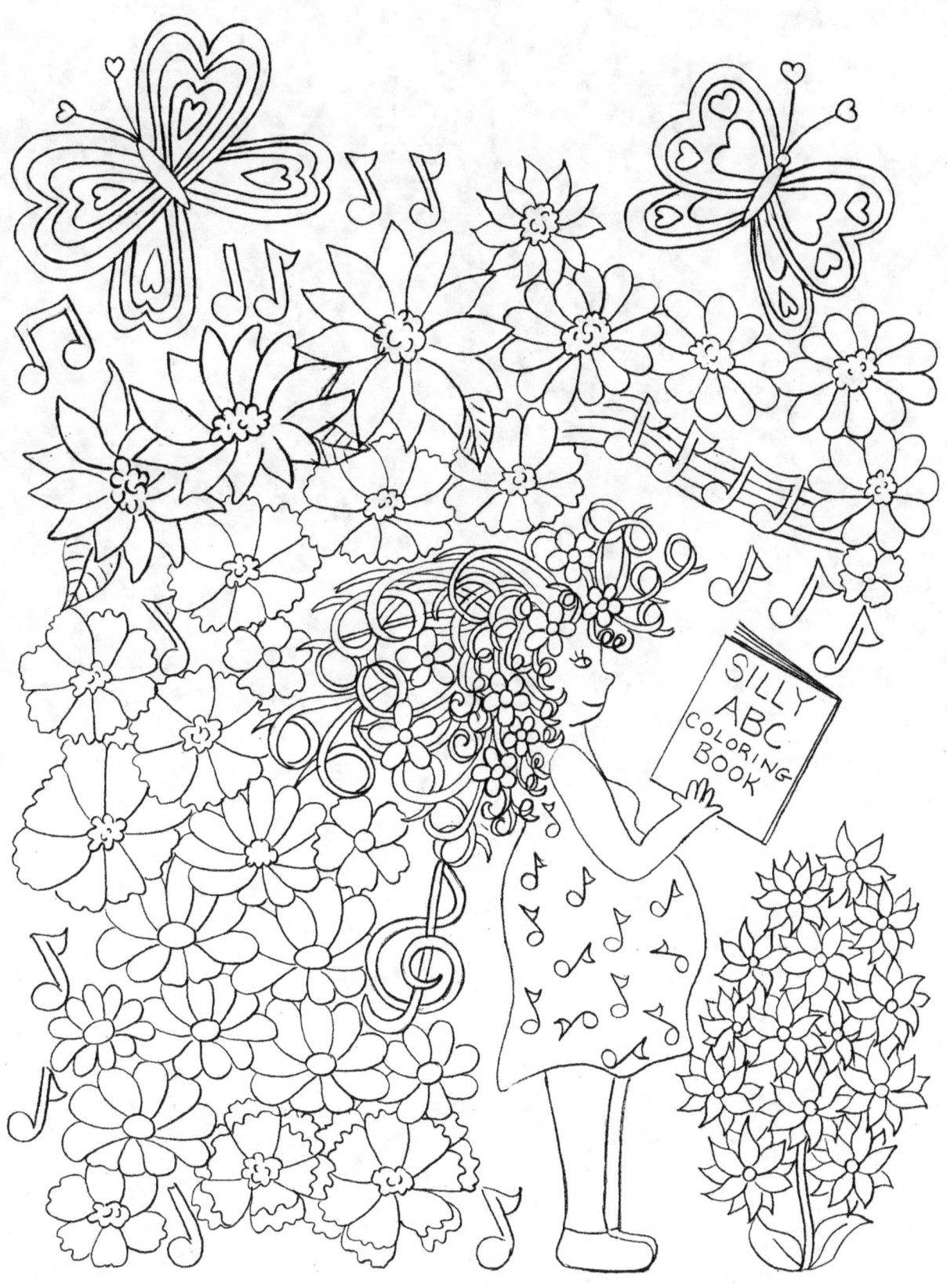

Dear Baby,

_____

_____

_____

_____

_____

_____

_____

_____

_____

_____

_____

_____

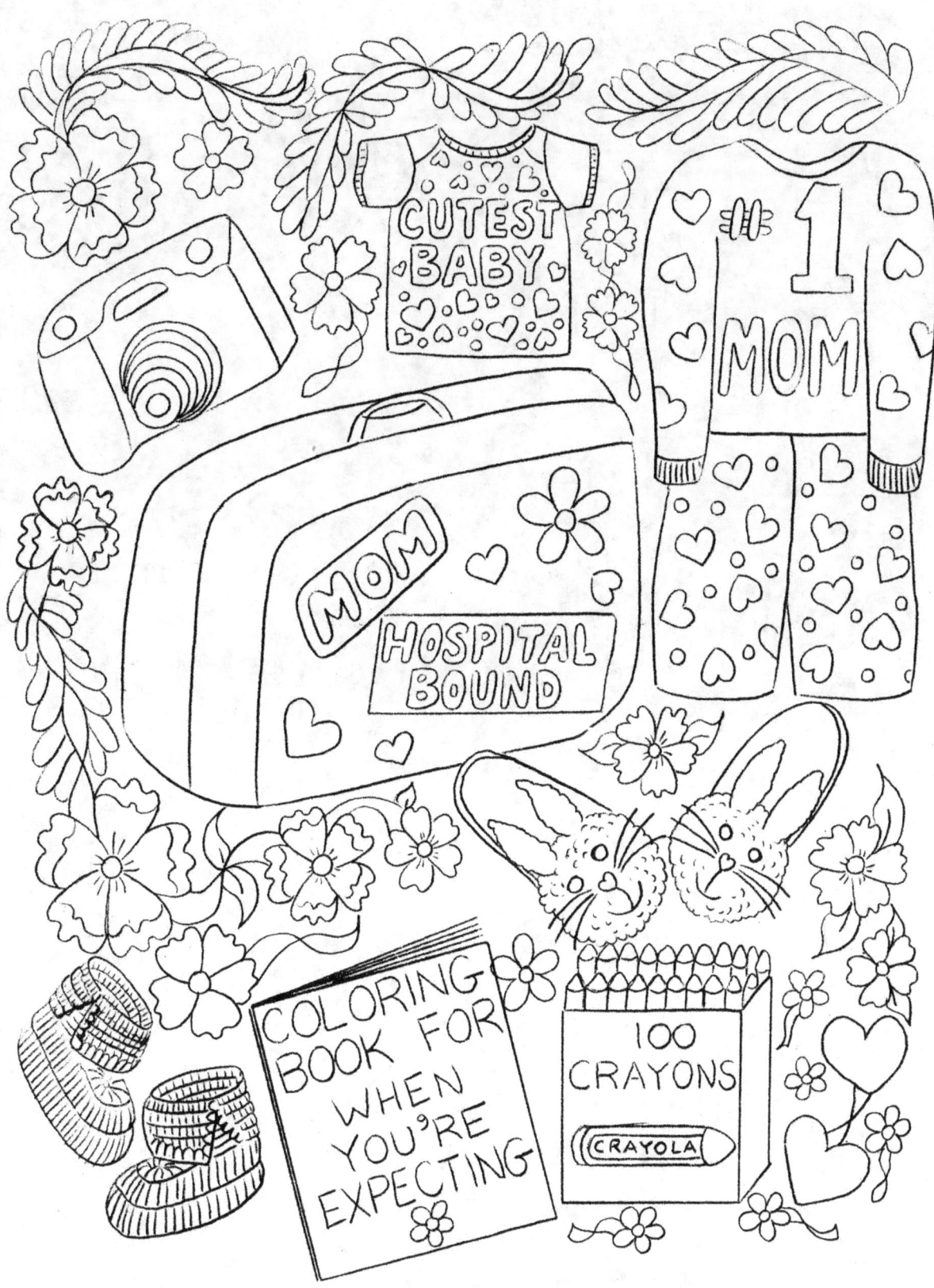

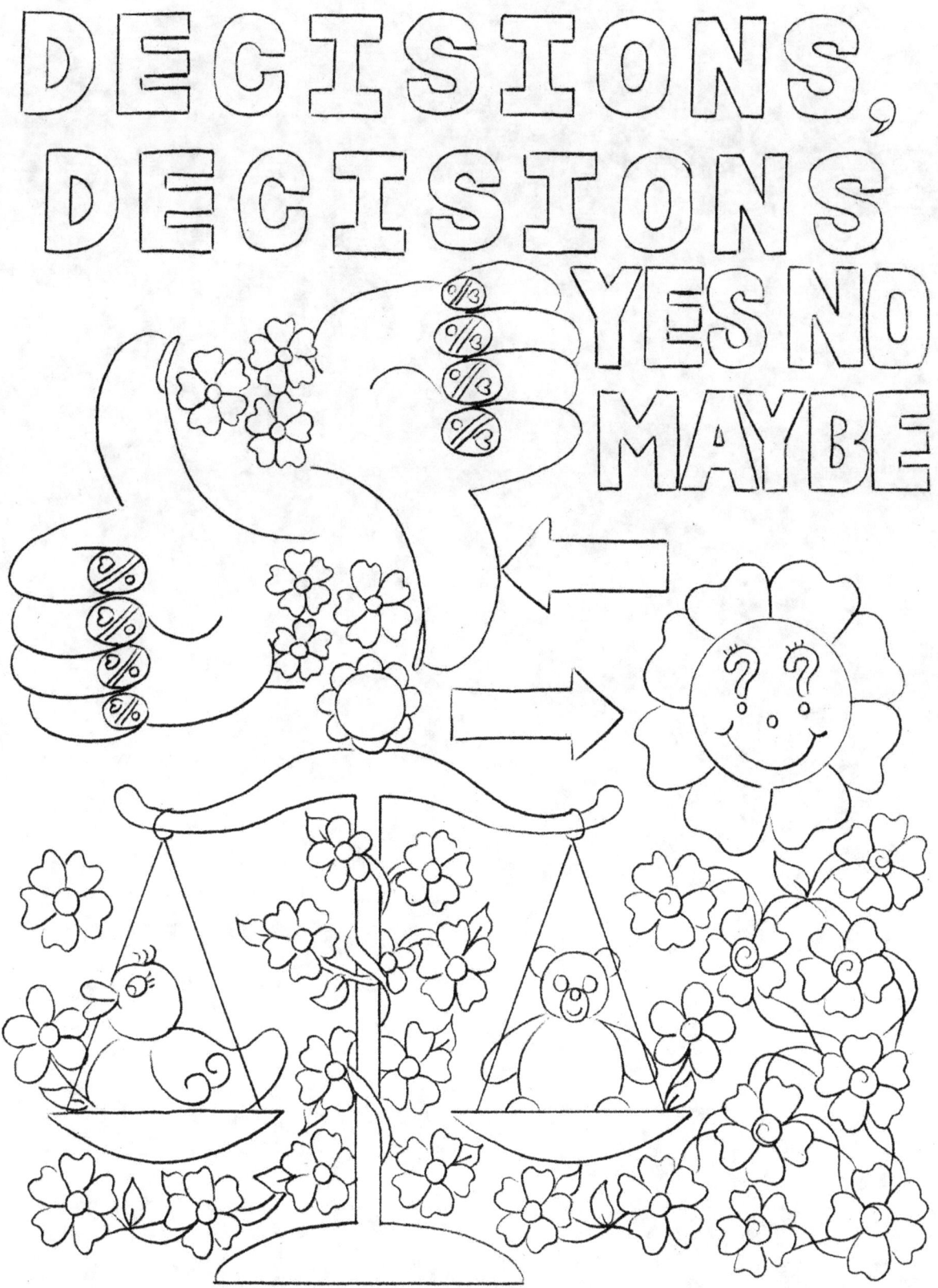

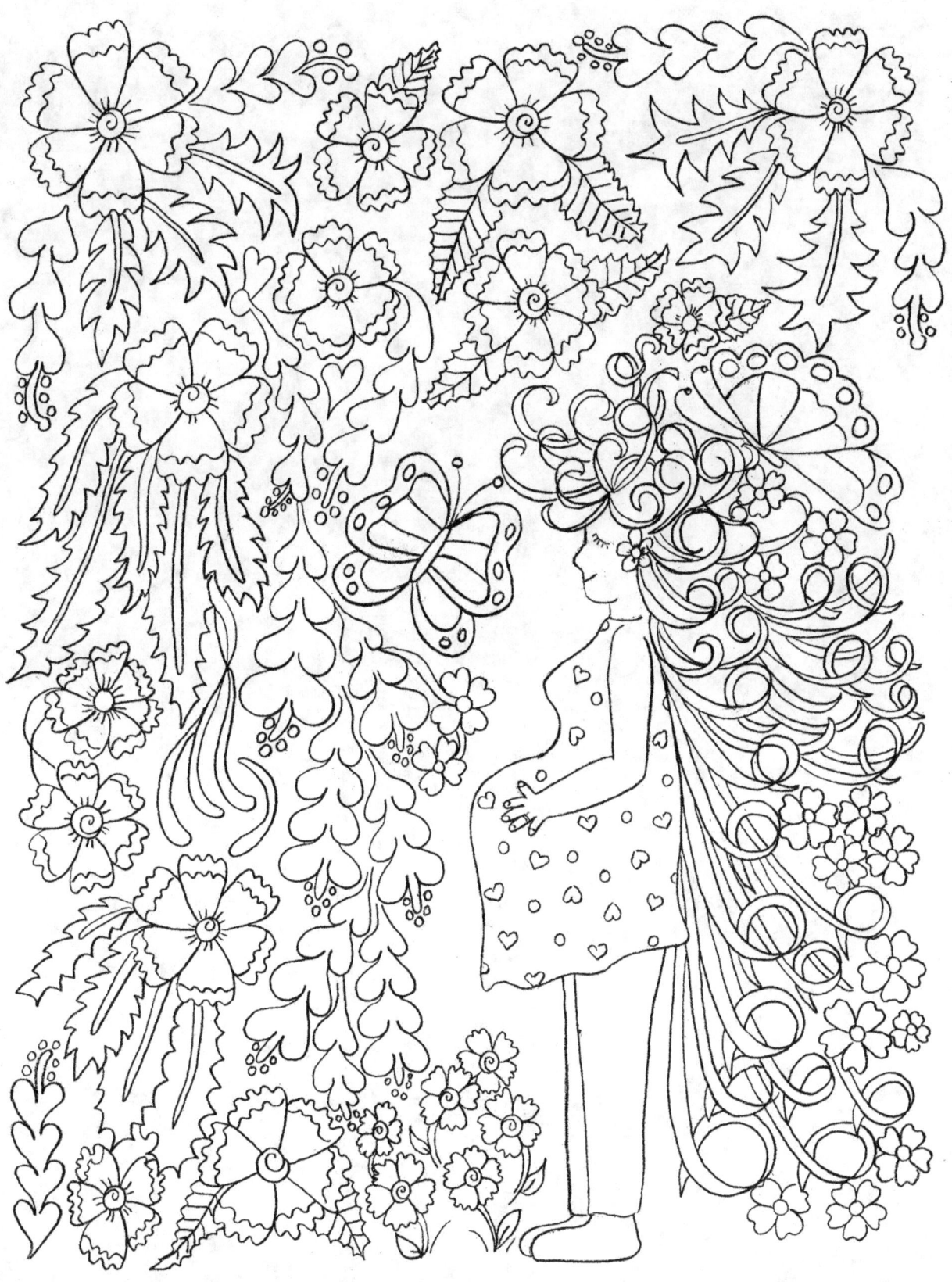

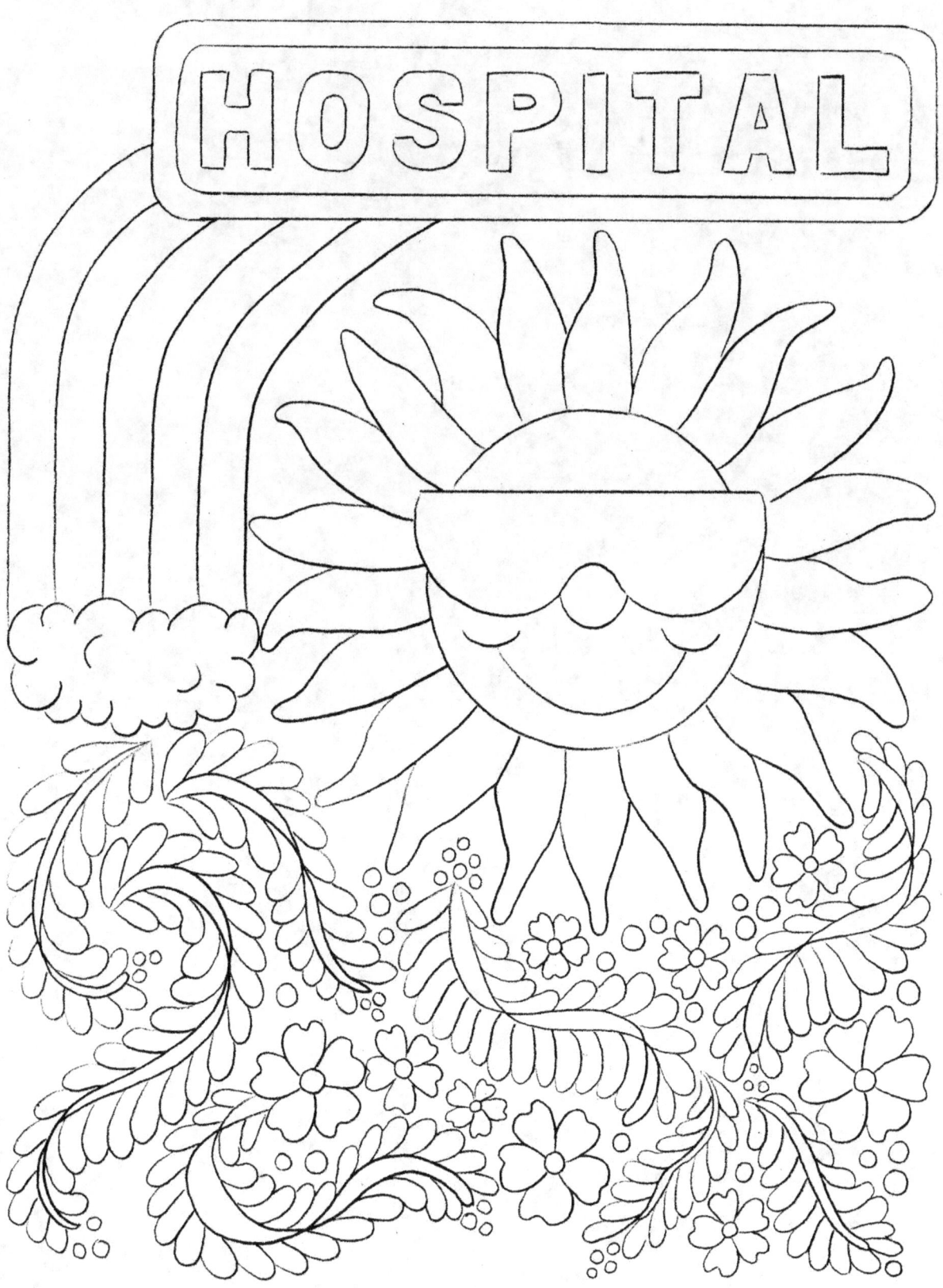

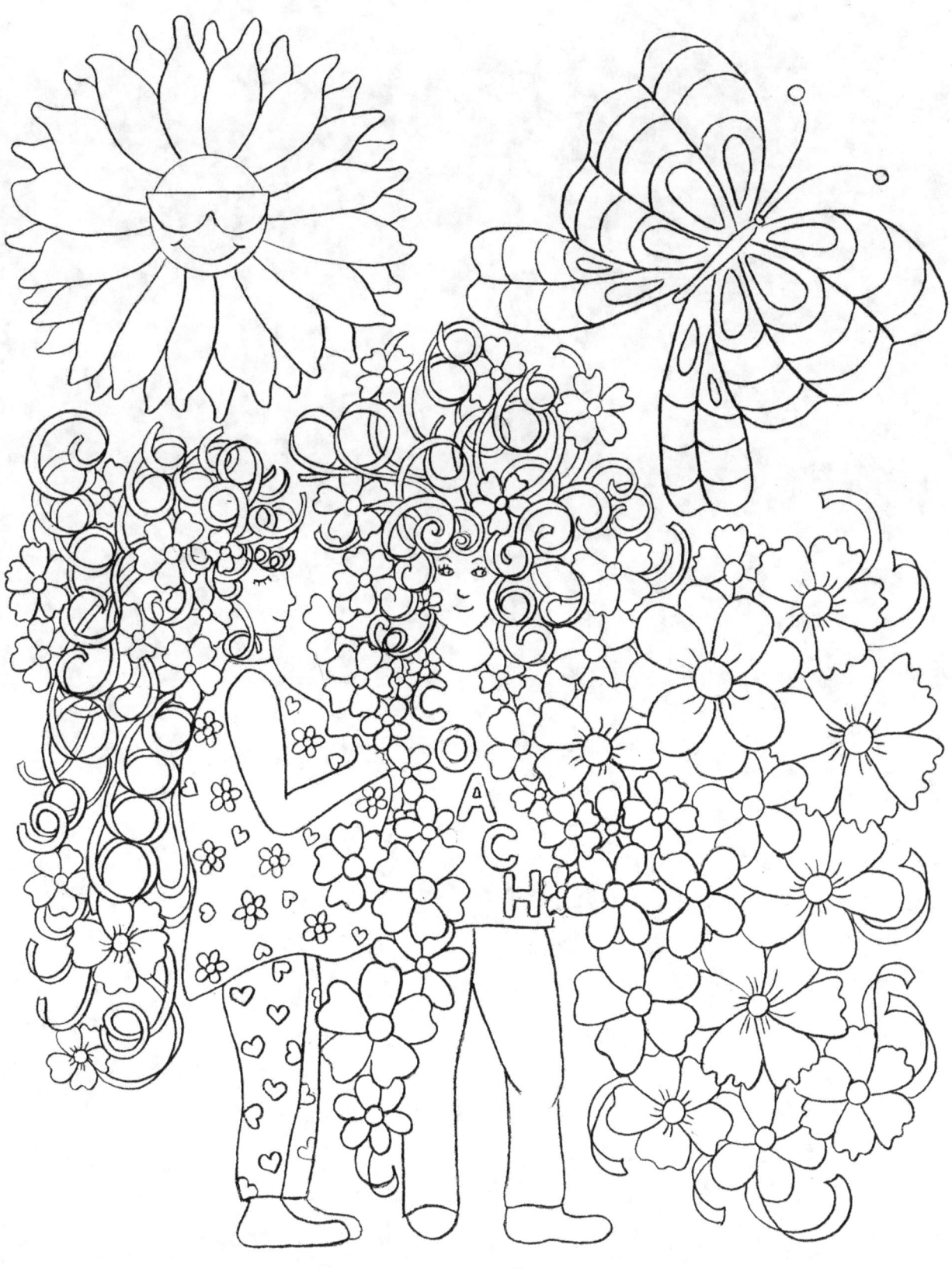

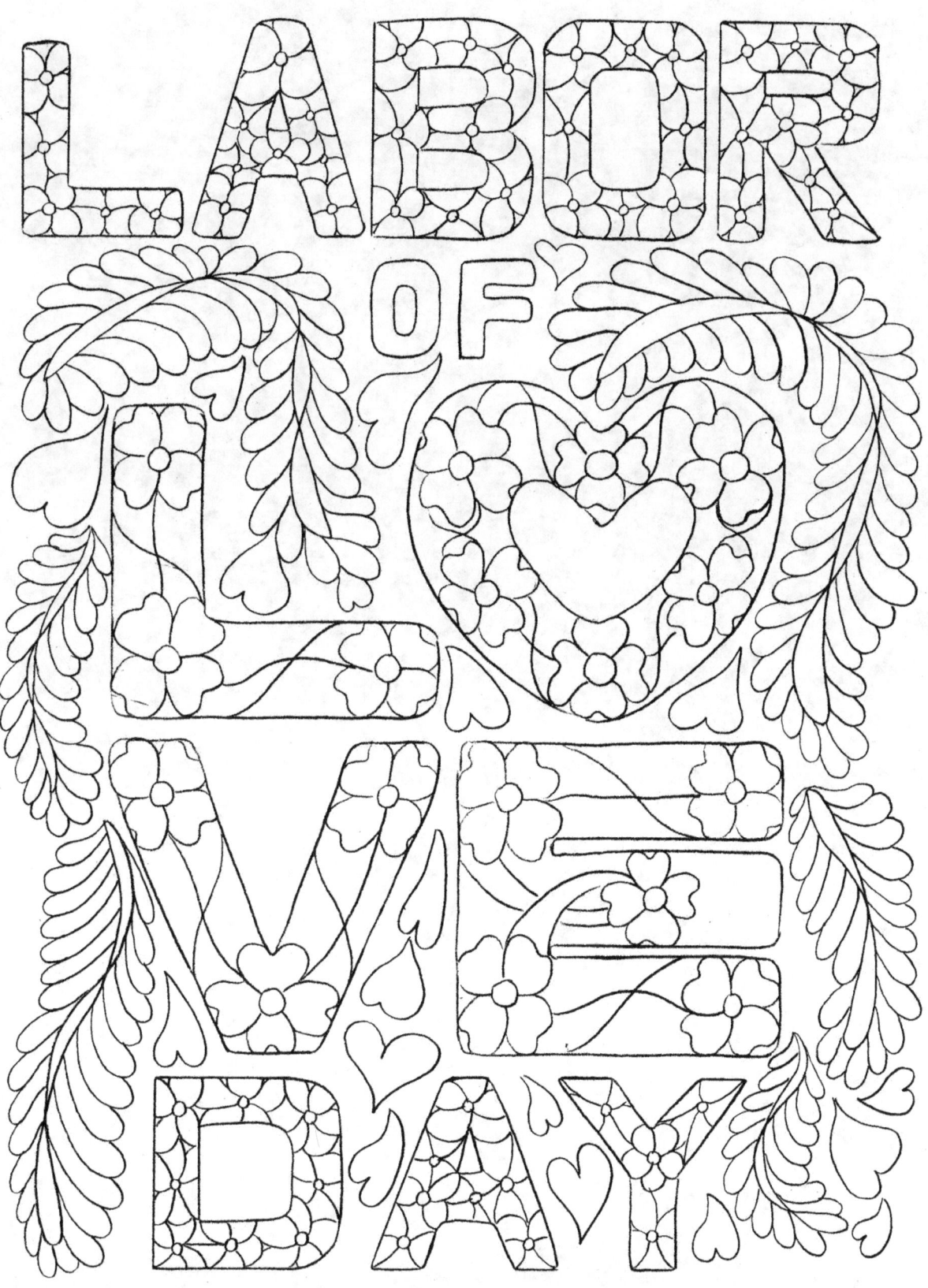

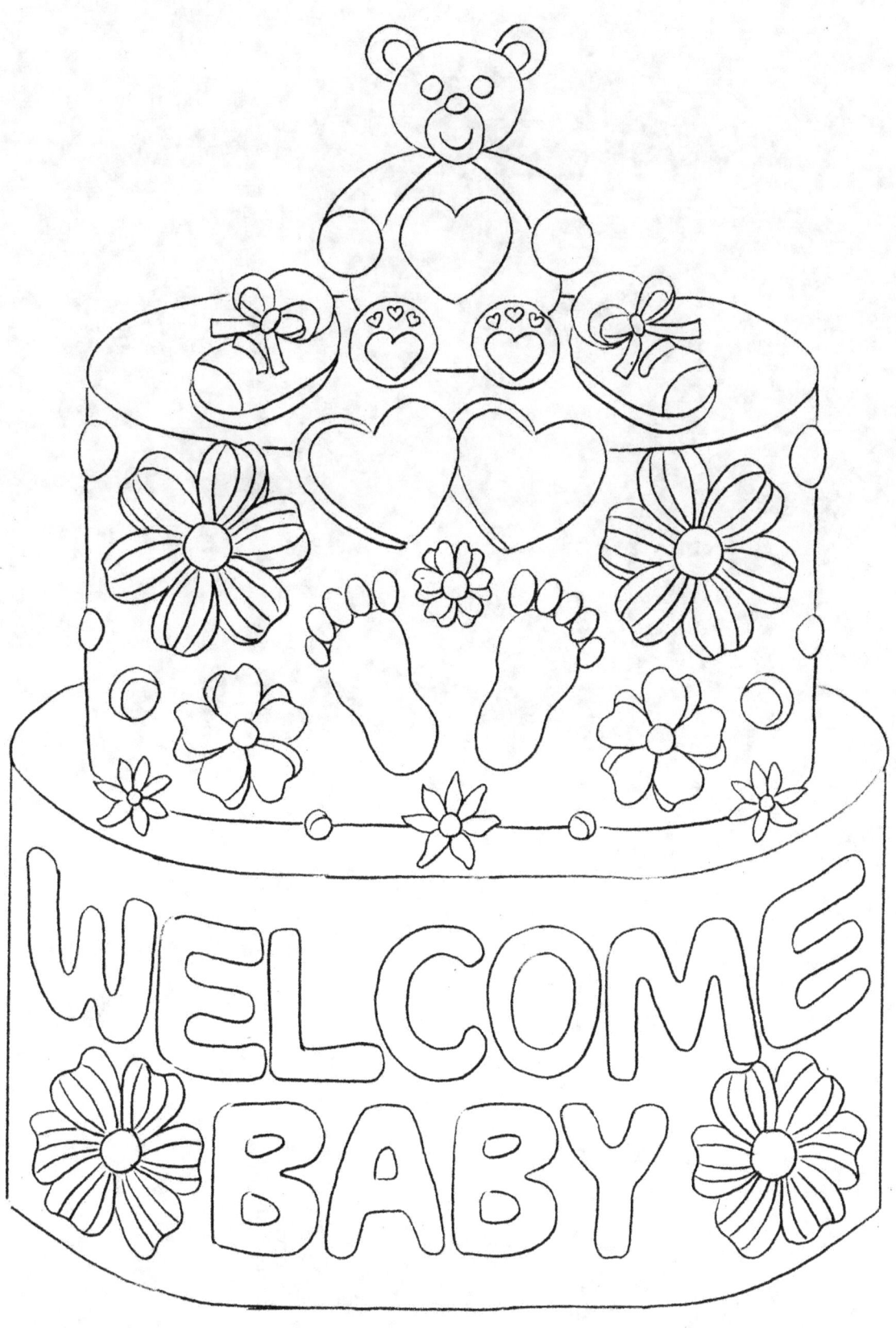

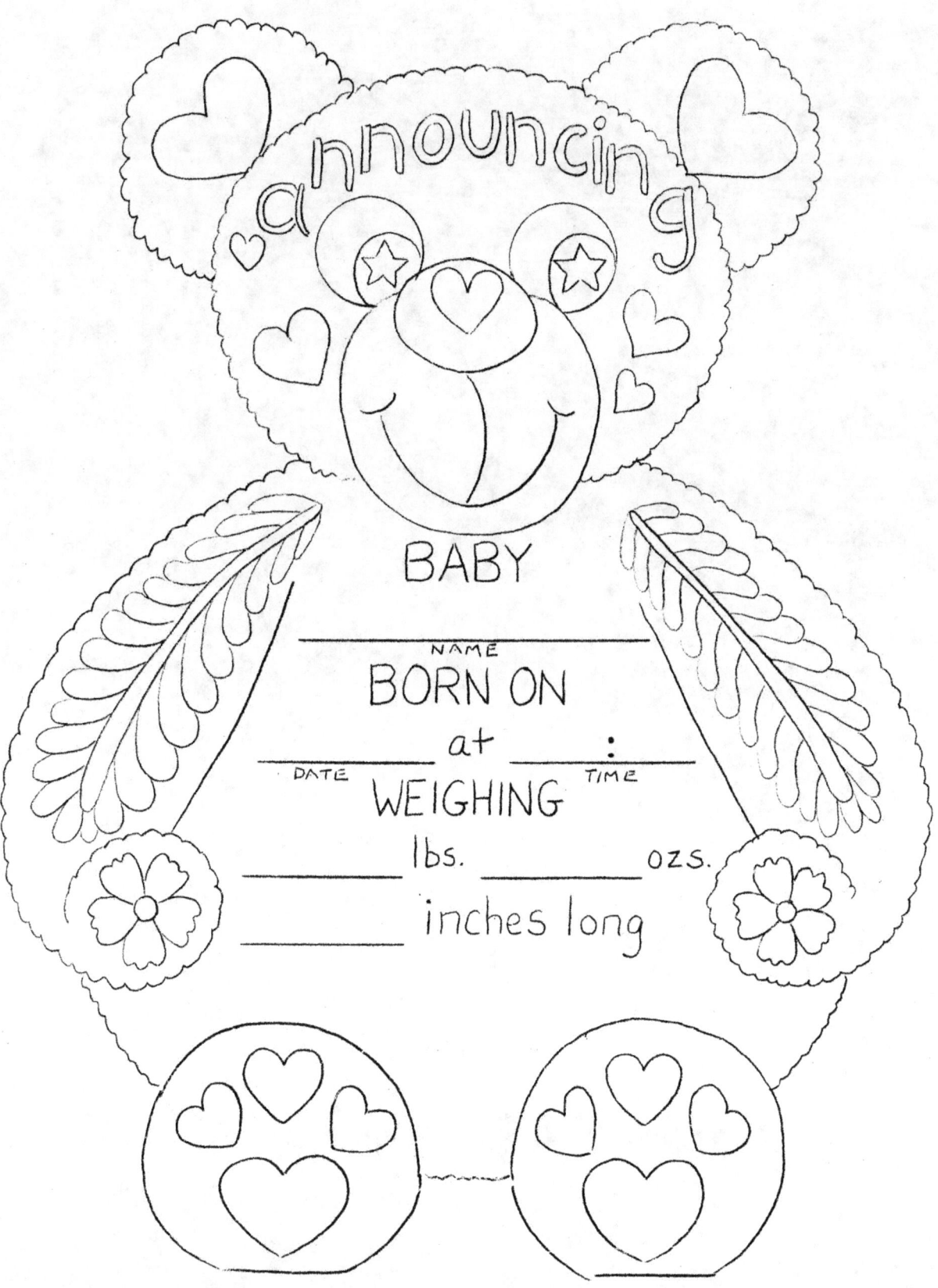

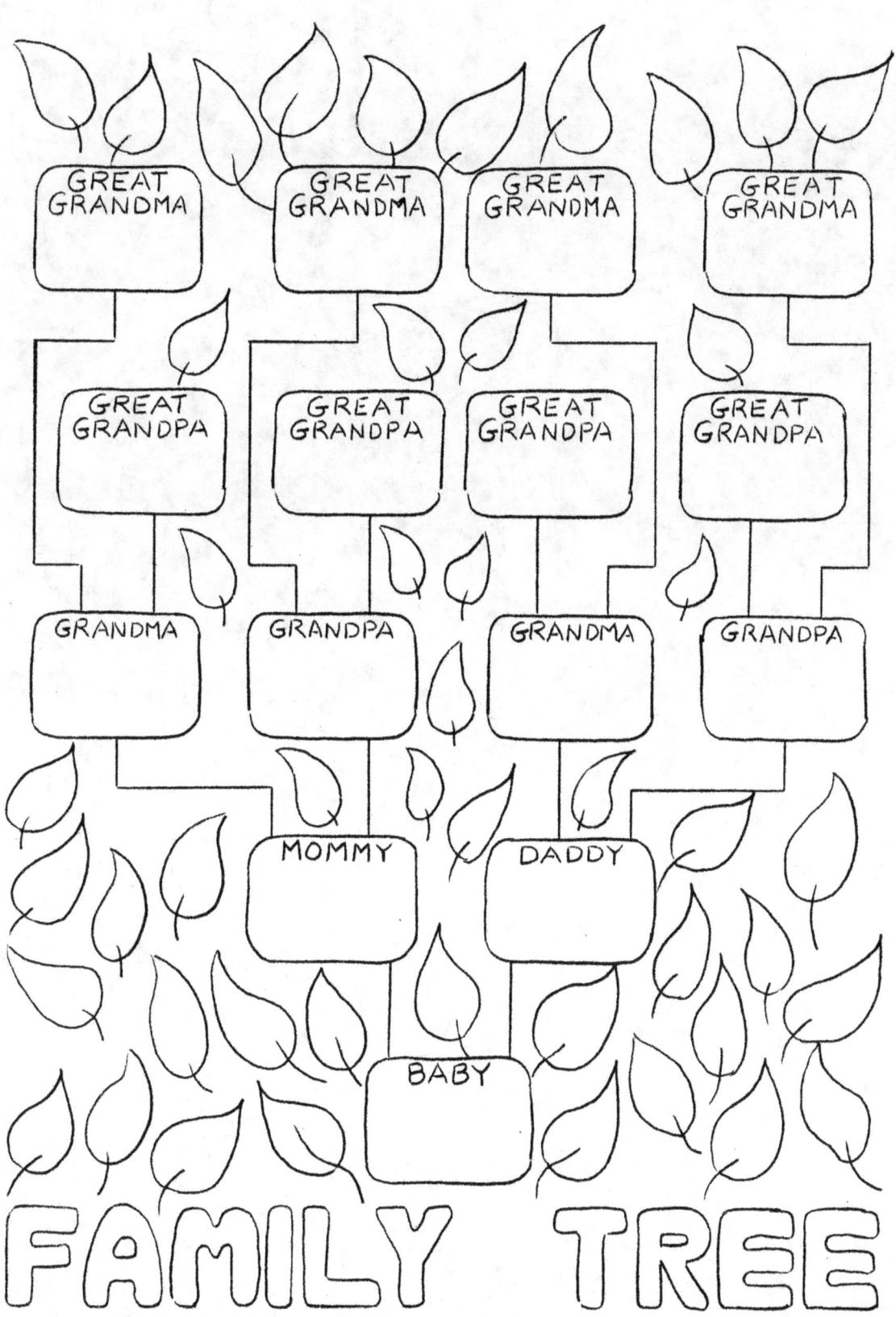

FAMILY TREE

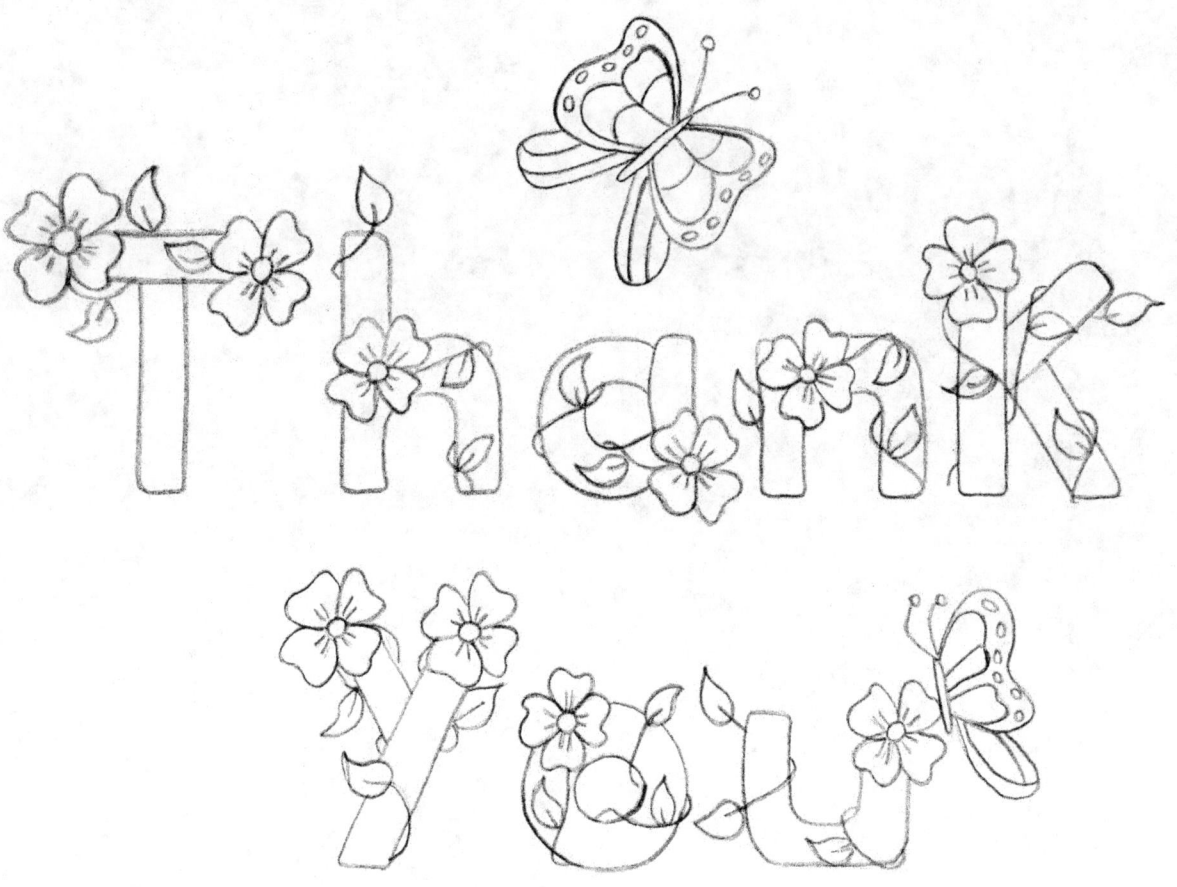